Mamma Mia!

Published by ECW Press
2120 Queen Street East, Suite 200, Toronto, Ontario, Canada M4E 1E2

NATIONAL LIBRARY OF CANADA CATALOGUING IN PUBLICATION

Mamma mia!: good Italian girls talk back / Maria Coletta McLean, ed.

ISBN 1-55022-652-5

1. Italian Canadian women — Anecdotes. I. McLean, Maria Coletta, 1946–

FC106.I8M43 2004   305.48'851071   C2004-902168-0

Editing: Joy Gugeler
Cover and Text Design: Tania Craan
Production and Typesetting: Mary Bowness
Printing: St. Joseph Print Group

This book is set in Minion.

The publication of *Mamma Mia!* has been generously supported by the Canada Council, the Ontario Arts Council, the Government of Canada through the Book Publishing Industry Development Program. **Canadä**

DISTRIBUTION
CANADA: Jaguar Book Group, 100 Armstrong Avenue, Georgetown, ON, L7G 5S4
UNITED STATES: Independent Publishers Group, 814 North Franklin Street, Chicago, Illinois 60610

PRINTED AND BOUND IN CANADA

ECW PRESS
ecwpress.com

Mamma Mia!

Good
Italian Girls
Talk Back

Collected by
Maria Coletta McLean

ECW PRESS

Table of Contents

Introduction

MARIA COLETTA MCLEAN

When I was nine, a wave of unknown cousins from my father's village of Supino immigrated to Toronto, adding Italian flavour to my Canadian lifestyle. They introduced me to the rules of acceptable behaviour for good Italian girls. Now, 77 years after my father landed at Pier 21 in Halifax, and 79 years after my mother arrived at Ellis Island in New York City, their youngest daughter is talking back, and I am not alone.

I am joined by 17 other women whose voices echo from coast to coast, across generations, and across the Atlantic. The collection includes women born in Canada or in Italy, women in their 20s to those in their 70s, from Victoria to Halifax and everywhere in between. We're Canadians, we're immigrants, we're storytellers, and we're proud of where we came from and where we're going. Our stories talk about saints and superstitions, weddings and funerals, Italian *paesani* and Canadian *mangiacakes*. Our stories are bound by a desire to speak truthfully and courageously about the traditions our ancestors have passed on to us and about the future we wish to build for ourselves. You have to be brave to be a writer, to put your words on the page for one and all, and this book belongs to that kind of writer. Welcome to a world in which good Italian girls talk back, a world that expands with each story to continue its conversation with you, the reader.

This book begins where many Italian festivities do, in the kitchen. In "Clever Little Compartments" I write about my mother who was always making homemade ravioli or gnocchi while I longed for that most un-Italian of entrées, a frozen TV dinner. My mother, like most good Italian mammas, didn't understand why she should buy prepared food when she could make it herself, so I had to take things into my own hands. This meant lying to my mother, changing my friend's name, disguising religious affiliations, and a host of other minor sins. *Mamma Mia!*

Maria Cioni's father cooked the Italian food in her family and in "Answering Rafaela" Maria tells her daughter the stories of Genesio Cioni's restaurant, La Villa. Maria's father prepared delicacies for the sisters of a neighbourhood nunnery, not to mention the sports heroes and other famous, and infamous, Calgarians who passed through his doors. Maria alternated between her German mother's home-cooked meals of meat and potatoes and her Italian father's menu of "spaghetti, rigatoni, penne, and ravioli" served at the restaurant. At La Villa good Italian food fought discrimination, raised funds, introduced a new culture, and brought comfort.

Netta Rondinelli's favourite food was Nutella and her sister Anabelle loved it too, but they had a mamma who would only buy one jar a week. In "Those Nutty Days Of Disco," Netta's sister also longs for a pair of blue jeans with heart shaped pockets, but Papa won't allow it so she steals a pair from the neighbour's clothesline. Rebel Netta watches with glee as the battles between her father and Anabelle escalate when Papa discovers the empty Nutella jar, the stolen jeans, and evidence of her mysterious *mangiacake* boyfriend. Netta wisely concludes, "Anabelle should have stolen her favourite food over the jeans with the heart-shaped pockets; at least she could have eaten it and gotten rid of the evidence."

Valerie Sovran Mitchell may not have wanted jeans as a teenager, but she did want a makeover: "long, fine, silver-blond hair . . . crystal-blue eyes . . . a perfect little turned up nose." In "Italian by a Nose," she bemoans the fact that she has "facial features that spring from the unadulterated Italian gene pools of my Abruzzese mother and my Friulano father — thick, dark hair which bends and curls in the presence of the slightest mist, deep brown eyes, and (how I used to cringe at the adjective) a Roman nose." In due time Valerie grows into her nose and her heritage and even plays a game with her children called *"niso, naso."*

As these good Italian girls grow up, they answer not only to their parents, but to the Catholic church. Luciana Ricciutelli writes in "Once a Catholic," "My mother used to tell me that God saw everything, and I mean *everything,* I did. She used to say it with a look that implied that He would then tell *her* everything." Confession was a nightmare for Luciana when at 7 she had to invent sins and at 17 she had to lie about them. Catholic beliefs, double standards, and guilt "got me to thinking, to asking questions that begged more questions" writes Luciana. Her story will have you asking questions, too.

The one question that a single Italian girl is always asked is, "When are you getting married?" Singledom, as Jennifer Febbraro identifies it, is a state rarely accepted by Italian relatives, especially the married ones. In "Apologia for Singledom" Jennifer establishes the hierarchy of the Italian-Canadian family and discovers unmarried women like herself dangerously close to the bottom of the heap. Like many women of her generation, Jennifer opts for an education, but is unable to explain her preference to her Italian-speaking grandmother. Most of their communication is mimed, and although it would be easy to tap the ring finger of the left hand to signal an engagement, Jennifer dares you to meet this challenge: "Try miming Ph.D."

If, like Jennifer, you choose to go to school instead of to the chapel, and then, to make matters worse, you move away from home, you are choosing a road less travelled. In Maria Montini's story, "Mamma," Maria's mother follows in the footsteps of all good Italian Mammas by collecting linens for her daughter's hope chest. But Maria is tempted by less traditional presents. "I entered school and discovered that the Anglo-Canadian girls got toys for Christmas rather than linens."

Next, Maria wanted books instead of toys, education instead of marriage, and an apartment instead of her mother's home. In the end, Maria decides that rather than move in next to her father, her father, two brothers, and dead mother would follow *her*.

Mothers can be challenging (as our title suggests) and while they don't usually push from beyond the grave, they do require a lot of attention. Things don't start off well in this respect for Maria Francesca LoDico and her mother in "An Affair To Remember," despite their attempt to talk with a therapist. "My mamma speaks Italian and a wee bit of French; Dr. Minde speaks only English. And so I found myself in a situation in which my mamma is very earnestly telling the therapist what she thinks is wrong with me — and I have to translate." Though her Italian mother's love sometimes feels like a stranglehold on Francesca's life, she does find a way to breathe and to share a few laughs in the process. After Aquafit classes and a shopping spree at the seafood counter, Francesca's mamma speaks her mind: "I'd like to be a nonna. I'm ready. But it's none of our business. No, no, none of our business, Fra. I'm not one of those overbearing mammas. No, no, that's not me." Still, Mamma has a plan devised for "a daughter in love, truly in love, with her mamma."

In "Thicker Than Water," Anna Nobile also has translation problems when it comes to communicating with her mother, but it's not a language barrier; it is her mother's inability to accept Anna's sexual preference. As a child Anna loved hearing the family stories as she and her mother sifted through the shoebox of black-and-whites. Now Anna is missing from those photos. To remedy the absence, she creates imaginary snapshots from her new home in Vancouver and inserts her widowed mother into a family joined not by blood but by love.

Though this romantic love doesn't always lead to marriage, the life of the Italian single girl still manages to involve a lot of weddings. Netta Rondinelli shows us a 12-year-old's view of her sister's wedding in "Anabelle's Dumb Wedding." First the elation: "This was finally my chance to be in a bridal party;" then the despair: "Under the pink tab for Bridesmaids, there are four similar sounding names — cousin Angela, cousin Angie, his cousin Angela, and Angelica — but no mention of mine." In a house where Mama and Papa are too *"preoccupati"* with the wedding plans to listen to Netta's complaints, Netta sabotages the preparations for her sister's wedding before experiencing a rite of passage of her own.

Weddings are meant to be a blessing for the family,

but occasionally the family strikes back, with a curse or two. If a jealous relative has done this to you, Ivana Barbieri knows the antidote: ". . . assume the defensive position. Middle fingers and thumbs curled in, forefinger and baby finger extended. You mess with the bull, you get the horns." If you're "Messing with the *Malocchio*" you're messing with the evil eye, but be warned, there are as many remedies as there are regions in Italy. A simple headache can be cured with medication, but Ivana's aunt assures us, "You can't cure a *malocchio* headache with Tylenol."

What would an Italian wedding be without the "Ave Maria," red roses, roasted chicken, and cannelloni? Nancy Kindy answers these questions and many more in her story, "Four Weddings and a Funeral." From 1941 to present day she traces the wedding traditions that have defined four generations, from her parents' simple reception at her grandmother Miraglia's house in Mimico to her son's wedding banquet in Barrie. And, naturally, arguments abound. Heather, the bride, wants roasted chicken but Uncle Domenic doesn't eat chicken; Steve, the groom, suggests a cash bar; Nancy, the mother, is tired of pasta and wants roast beef. When the discussions around the dinner table get heated, non-Italian Steve observes, "My family doesn't even talk during dinner."

Francesca Schembri explores another wedding tradition, the arranged marriage. She also takes us back to Italy and back in time with, "Like Pigs to Slaughter." Here a young bride without a dowry sits by the wayside as wedding plans are made for her. Gone is her dream of romantic love, a white wedding gown, a home near her widowed mother. Instead, she is sacrificed so that her family can be spared from poverty and disgrace. As she walks to the church she compares herself to a pig about to be slaughtered, "crying loudly as it was dragged toward the butcher block," and reminds herself that the pig's death is necessary for the family to survive.

Rosanna Battigelli's story provides "Food for Thought" in a scenario that takes marital unhappiness one step further and invokes both anger and disappointment from a mother ashamed to admit her daughter's divorce. As they make sausages the daughter realizes her mamma "may have adopted a new country 40 years ago . . . but she remained in Italy emotionally." The story serves up an unexpected slice of humble pie in the last line of a tale that reminds us reconciliation comes in many flavours.

But once a good Italian girl gets married (assuming she *stays* married) she must get on with the blessed duty of having children, preferably boys. In "May You Have

Many Sons," Angela Capozzolo asks "What made boys the favoured progeny?" Her parents had many rules of conduct for a good Italian girl but Angela observes that, "Boys did not need to say thank you or please. They did not need to sit and endure hours of adult conversation. They could eat as many cookies as they desired. . . ." Angela's parents encourage their daughter to get an education first and get married second, but Angela soon discovers that the struggle for a more egalitarian household means an uphill battle. Angela and her husband are blessed with two children. You guessed it: boys.

The opposite of a blessing has to be a curse, a hex easy enough to laugh off if it weren't for stories like Luciana Ricciutelli's "Full." Luciana writes, "I come from a long line of women whose curses bind them together." Luciana's grandmother curses her beloved son in a moment of anger and the women in her family bear the consequences: "I curse you . . . so that one day you too will have a daughter who will leave you!" Luciana's mother curses her with, "May you never be happy one day in your life!" How does Luciana, who now has a daughter of her own, plan to break the chain?

Curses are not the only things passed on from generation to generation; there is also the weight of a surname passed from parent to child. In "What's in a

Name?" Maria Cioni returns to her father Genesio's first restaurant in Calgary called GENE'S SPAGHETTI PARLOR. The newspaper ad for its opening called it JEANE'S SPAGHETTI PARLOR. A partnership changes the name again to GENE'S SPAGHETTI DINE & DANCE, but when the partnership sours Genesio discovers the true worth of a name he built as much as inherited. Against the backdrop of World War II the Canadian government adds a third moniker to her mother's German name and her father's Italian one: "enemy alien."

In "Italian By Choice," Carrie-Ann Smith is equally conflicted about her identity; though her name is not the half of it, not even a quarter. Though she writes about growing up "in the warm centre of a ravioli universe" she can't speak Italian except for swear words and eventually arrives at the shocking realization that she is less than 25 per cent Italian. "We didn't have a kitchen in our base-ment; our house wasn't in the West End; and cruellest of all, my mother made spaghetti sauce from a can — the less said the better." As Carrie-Ann reviews her past and chronicles her present, she discovers a universal truth: "So we tell our stories and we become that which we love." With an un-Italian surname like Smith and a love of all things Italian, Carrie-Ann comes up with her own answer to, "What's in a name?"

Sometimes you have to go home to know where you came from, as Angela Capozzolo learns during a trip to Italy as a young girl, travelling to her father's birthplace and recording those memories in her story, "Bellos-guardo." Standing before the house where he was born, Angela's father "asked the current tenants if he could show his daughters his childhood home. His eyes were full of tears as he took us room to room telling 25 years of memories." Meanwhile, Angela corrects the villagers who call she and her sister *Americane*, in between gorging on gelato, haunting graveyards, and lounging on the Amalfi Coast. Upon her return to school in September, she recognizes that her vacation has done more than expand her vocabulary, it has affected her identity: "When lunch arrived, I was not ashamed of taking out my *panino con prosciutto cotto e bocconcini* from my lunch bag. I never begged my mother for peanut butter and jam sandwiches again. And, most importantly, on Parent-Teacher Night, my parents' Italian accent did not cause me any grief."

In "Riding the Rails," Ivana Barbieri takes us across Italy by train, a postscript to her first visit to Calabria with her mother, sister, and aunt 11 years earlier. As a single woman travelling alone she meets a variety of passengers including a letch, a drug addict, a prostitute, a nun, and a sailor. She sleeps in one-star hotels, negotiates customs, endures pick-up lines, and contemplates joining a convent, but only momentarily: *"Who am I kidding? I can't live without Shoppers Drug Mart, much less flirting or bikini waxes."*

In "The View From Here" Giselle Signoroni compares her parents' Italian home in a "village worthy of first kisses and last rites" to her childhood Toronto apartment. Unlike many of us who longed to fit in, Giselle "longed to fit the stereotype, to have an identity, to have parents who had a mortgage rather than a lease, who drank wine and not whiskey, who canned tomatoes and made biscotti, who held big celebrations with families and friends." Giselle writes of the privilege of being at home in two countries and belonging to both. "The meaning of my past, like everyone's past, is forever changing. The definition of my village, my family, my life now, is relative to what it once was and will be. Both homes, like lovers, give me a sense of, a view of, myself. The caresses and compliments, like breezes and showers, warm and cool me. My understanding depends on how much I allow myself to enjoy my surroundings."

Mirella (Sichirollo) Patzer also returns to the mother country in "Down Three Steps," a phrase from a dream that directs her to the gravesite of her infant brother. "San

Leonardo is a small village and news travels fast," so the villagers know that Mirella is in search of ghosts and haunted by her mother's words: "I had never seen such a small white coffin. Your father carried it to the church by himself. He refused to allow anyone to help. The entire village followed behind us." On a day when "my mamma's past had become my present," Mirella honours her mother's request and finds more than a gravestone.

Carla Maria Lucchetta's story also involves the death of a sibling. Eleven years separate she and her sister, but everyone says they look so alike. In "The Vigil," 14-year old Carla suspects something's wrong when the relatives start calling for her mother in the middle of the day. When Carla is finally told that her older sister has died, she's also given this advice: "If you need to cry, do it now, because your mother is going to need you to be strong." Carla observes her silent mother in prayer and wonders why the secrecy her parents use to protect her has rendered everyone mute. The story is an ode to her sister and to the love that defies unanswered questions.

In "Talking Pictures," Francesca Schembri spins her own tale of loss in a widow's story so heart-wrenching that we can barely listen to it unfold, yet we cannot turn away. We hear the widow Carmelina talking to her long-dead husband about their maiden voyage to Canada as newlyweds: "To get some privacy, we used to sneak out at night. One of those nights, while the watchful sea serenaded us, our son was conceived." That son does the family proud by becoming a lawyer, but he changes his name: "Your son was not Vincenzo Di Martino, but Vince St. Martin! Forgive him, *gioia mia*." Carmelina also tells her husband about their daughter, Santina, who met a *mangiacake* boyfriend and moved in with him. Carmelina fears people will attribute Santina's conduct to the fact that she didn't have a father and disapprove of the way she has raised Santina, so she makes a tragic decision that threatens both her daughter's life and her own.

In Rosanna Battigelli's second story, "In Living Colour," the bonds that bind father and daughter reach across the darkness. As Rosanna watches her father's body deteriorate as Parkinson's disease threatens his sight she "thinks about the colour being leached from his life, fading like a photograph exposed to too much sunlight," and recalls the family photos that have silently recorded their history. The priest has already murmured "the appropriate prayers for the family," but Rosanna has her own prayer, one strong enough to light his way.

The women of *Mamma Mia!* hope that these stories will light the path to a brighter future for all of us as we continue our dialogue with each other and with you. We invite you to read on and to share the stories that are as courageous as the ancestors — Canadian, Italian, or otherwise — who inspired them.

Maria Coletta McLean
Toronto, April 2004

Clever Little Compartments

MARIA COLETTA MCLEAN

Even as I unpacked the boxes, I knew I wouldn't like living in our brand new bungalow in Weston. I hated the cement sidewalks, the paved streets, the neatly landscaped yards. In Humber Summit, I had skated on Castator's pond, sledded down old lady Tansley's hill, cut through the cemetery at dusk. With my cousins, I had marched through the rows of my Uncle Fidel's rye field and collected pop bottles in the ditches to trade in for blackballs at Evan's store. I couldn't do any of those things here. And I missed my friends. It was like moving from Mayberry into Leave it To Beaver's house. My mother assured me I'd get use to it. "You'll make new friends," she said.

But Bobbi Lancaster was like all the other girls in Weston. She had twin sweater sets in different colours and when she tossed the cardigan off her shoulders, the label said "Kitten." Her father was a schoolteacher, not just a regular teacher, but a university professor. My father was a truck driver for Toronto Macaroni. My uncles were cement workers, excavators, labourers. My mother was a housewife, but Bobbi's mother belonged to some club called the Junior League and every Wednesday she went to something called a Luncheon Meeting and Bobbi was allowed to go home alone. She had a key, which she kept in her purse, and each week she invited a friend for lunch. When she asked me, I had to think fast. I didn't want to admit that my mother would never let me go to Bobbi's house if her mother wasn't home. I could imagine reasoning with my mother, "I'm in Grade 8. All the other kids' mothers allow them to . . ." but I knew she wouldn't budge.

I opened my mouth to say no, but at that moment

Bobbi added these seductive words, "My mother's leaving TV dinners for us." Well, that did it. I had longed for TV dinners ever since we'd bought our television. There was no chance I was ever going to get a TV dinner at home; I'd asked enough times to know that. My mother didn't understand the concept of buying prepared food when she could make it herself. Although I could usually wear her down if I wanted something badly enough, I was not making any headway. It made no sense to her and I had run out of arguments. So I lied to my mother, told her my friend's name was Roberta because it sounded more Italian, swore Roberta's mother would be home, and after I was drilled in the daily routine of washing my hands with soap before I ate, folding the towel the same way I found it, asking if I could help, carrying my plate to the counter, remembering to say thank-you, I was allowed to go.

Roberta lived on King Street. It was lined with old maple trees so we walked down the sidewalk scrunching the leaves.

"How long will it take to cook the TV dinner?" I asked.

"They're already in the oven, silly."

"But I thought your mother was out."

"She is. The oven's on automatic. Everything will be ready when we get there."

I mulled over the magic of a preset oven and a mother who had everything ready. My mother expected me to set the table, help with the food, and wash the dishes. I was so lost in these thoughts I almost walked past Bobbi's house. We walked up the cement driveway, past the leaded glass windows of the main floor and around to the side door. As soon as Bobbi opened the door, I could smell the dinner baking. Inside, the table was set with place mats, another thing we didn't have at our house. They were plastic. All you had to do was wipe them off with a damp rag. They were nothing like the heavy damask tablecloth my mother insisted on using, the one with the matching napkins I had to iron, one by one, until I thought I'd scream.

"Two more minutes," said Bobbi. "Want to see the rest of the house? Come on, I'll show you the library."

I didn't know regular people had libraries in their own houses, but Bobbi did. Two walls were covered with mahogany shelves lined with hardcover books. Mahogany wood was something I knew all about because my mother bought a mahogany dining room set when we'd moved into the new house. It was part of my Saturday morning chores to dust the carved legs and polish the brass toe caps. The bookshelves in Bobbi's library exuded a faint scent of lemon oil and dust. My mother said dust was the enemy of a clean house. A bell chimed.

"Lunch is ready. Coke or ginger ale?" she asked.

"Coke," I replied casually, pretending I was allowed to drink pop with my meals at home. We had had to drink milk ever since my teacher sent home that Canada's Food Guide; my mother had taped it to the inside of the cupboard. Bobbi sat two Coke bottles on the table, no glasses. She slipped her hands into oven mitts and slid the TV dinners out of the oven. They were smaller than I expected, but the shiny aluminum made them look like gifts just begging to be opened. Inside were clever little compartments separating the mashed potatoes from the bright green peas and the meat.

"Mmm," sighed Roberta. "Chicken's my favourite. I love the stuffing."

So it was *chicken* beneath the anemic gravy. It tasted okay, not great, but all right. The peas were gone in three forkfuls and the potatoes — well, they were the real surprise. Soap flakes whipped together with skim milk. In my mouth, they slowly dissolved into nothing — no flavour, no texture, just potato-scented air. I drank my Coke, tried not to burp, and wondered if there was anything else to eat.

Following Bobbi's lead, I stuffed the aluminum tray into the garbage bag. Next she brought out a box of chocolate cupcakes. Each one was packaged in a cellophane wrapper and topped with a thick layer of dark icing. Inside was a centre of cream that tasted not unlike the mashed potatoes.

"I have an aunt named Regina — that means Queen in Italian — and she makes this chocolate cake whenever we go to her house. She leaves it right in the pan she baked it in and ices it with cocoa and icing sugar and cream. The icing's almost as thick as the cake and across the top she runs a fork to make a crisscross pattern. Sometimes she shells some walnuts and sprinkles them on top."

"That's pretty old fashioned. My mother says the modern woman doesn't waste her time making things from scratch."

"That's what I try to tell my mother, but she seems to *like* being old-fashioned."

After lunch we sat in Roberta's yard under an old maple tree. The grass was neatly trimmed and the rose gardens had borders. Across the back of the yard ran a picket-style fence — tall boards with no spaces between them. I thought about the riotous vegetable garden we had in our yard, the tomato stakes made from scrap wood, the zucchini hanging on chicken wire vines, the apricot trees fighting for space with the roaming vegetable marrow plants, and the wild cosmos sprouting up wherever they could put down roots.

∼

My mother was standing at the door when I arrived home that day instead of in the kitchen where I usually found her.

"How was your lunch?" she asked as I stepped in the door.

"Great," I lied. "TV dinners are great."

On my way through the kitchen, I pulled off the end of the Italian bread and slipped the loaf back in the paper bag. As I stuffed the crusty heel into my mouth, I spied the ravioli my mother had made that afternoon. Usually we made it together, my mother rolling the dough, spooning out the filling and slicing it into squares, while I pressed the edges together with the tines of a fork. Ravioli was really a Sunday meal because it took most of the afternoon to make and required a large floured space, like the kitchen table, to sit before it was boiled and topped with tomato sauce. Usually I complained loudly about having to help with this chore, so today I was happy to see my favourite pasta already prepared.

When the ravioli was boiling in the pot, my mother wiped off the kitchen table and quickly lowered the tablecloth. After I set the table, I brought the pop bottle from the pantry and poured the wine from it into my father's glass.

"At Roberta's house, they have pop with their meals."

"Hmmm," said my mother.

"At Roberta's house, they have plastic place mats. All you have to do is wipe them off."

"Hmmm," said my mother.

"And with TV dinners, you can throw the container away afterwards. No dishes to wash."

"Hmm," said my mother.

"And you can buy little cakes that come in cellophane and they're already iced."

"The cheese," reminded my mother. Grating the cheese was usually my dad's job, but he had come home late tonight and was still washing. The grating had to be done at the last minute because my mother claimed the cheese kept its flavour better that way. When my father did it, he always grated a small mountain of cheese onto a piece of wax paper and then funnelled it into a glass bowl. Whenever I did it, I grated a knuckle or two in my hurry to get the job done and after I was finished I'd have to bandage my finger.

"You know you can buy cheese already grated. It comes in a cardboard box."

"Yes, cardboard," said my mother.

I thought back to the taste of those mashed potatoes, that taste that I couldn't quite define. Cardboard was pretty close.

"Roberta wants me to go to a girls' club with her on Monday evening."

"Monday's a school night."

"It's at the church. I'd be home by nine. Her father's going to pick me up."

"I don't . . ."

"It's at the church," repeated my father. "Let her go."

I neglected to mention that Bobbi's church was the local *United* church, not the Catholic church where we went every Sunday. I also left out the part about taking your own dinner. That weekend I devised a plan to prepare my own dinner — something Bobbi called a box lunch, as in, "Everyone brings their own box lunch." I envisioned a simple ham sandwich with mustard on Wonder bread and some store bought cookies. Maybe Oreos. My mother was always in the kitchen and even if I could manage to sneak out a few biscotti, an apple, there was still the problem of explaining why I wasn't eating at home. Finally, at five o'clock, half an hour before Bobbi's father was due to pick me up, I decided to tell the truth, or at least part of it.

"At this club, all the kids bring a lunch and eat together, sort of like a picnic."

"You eat outside?"

"No, we eat inside. But you don't need to make the lunch. I can do it."

My mother shook her head at the trio of strange ideas: eating lunch for dinner, a picnic inside a church hall, and the thought that I would prepare my own food. I didn't really know how to explain it to her. I only knew I wanted to fit in.

"You go and wash," she said. "I'll get the food ready."

I could hear her banging pots and dishes around in the kitchen as I repeated to myself, "Not scrambled egg and pepper sandwiches. Please, not meatball on a bun. Not prosciutto and provolone cheese."

Suddenly Bobbi's father was at the door, introducing himself to my mother, shaking her hand. "Something smells good," he said.

My mother just nodded and motioned me to the kitchen to show me the lunch.

"Hold your lunch on your lap. And don't forget to thank Mr. Lancaster."

She'd packed my lunch in a cardboard box and lifted the tea towel to show me the contents: a bowl of penne with tomato sauce, silverware rolled up in a napkin, a bunch of grapes, and a wax paper bundle held together with an elastic band.

"Ma, what's this?" I exclaimed, dreading the thought of carrying my lunch in a cardboard box with PRODUCT OF ITALY stamped on the side.

"The cheese. Already grated."

Answering Rafaela

MARIA CIONI

"When Mamma was a little girl," began every bedtime story I told my daughter, Rafaela, who snuggled closer to hear tales of my childhood. At first, the stories were short and simple, but by the time she was eight they had become something more.

In this way, my daughter learned the basics: Grandpa Genesio was born in Italy; his father died at a young age and his mother immigrated to Canada to remarry, leaving her two small sons with relatives; in 1923, at age 16, Genesio arrived in Calgary, having been sent for by his mother; Grandma Martha, an American, who spoke German and who adopted her husband's Italian culture with zeal; Genesio and Martha worked very hard to give my brother and me educational opportunities they never had. I lived above my parent's Italian restaurant, La Villa, where my birthday parties were held, much to the delight of my friends, most of whom had never eaten freshly prepared Italian food.

Over the years, Rafaela came to know her grandfather: a short, round, balding man with a warm smile and dark eyes twinkling with humour. He wore a fedora and gold watch and was impeccably dressed. Cars and jewelry were his weakness. He found pleasure in their craftsmanship and design — "Little works of art," he called them. He was "an immigrant who had made it." Looking successful made him acceptable in this new world.

"Why do people in Calgary remember Grandpa Gene?" asked Rafaela as she prepared her grade three assignment (to create a family history).

"Calgarians remember the tastes of Grandpa's food. For many, it was their first experience with Italian cuisine. La Villa was more than a restaurant, it was a meeting place. Between 1952 and 1958, people from every walk of life gathered to enjoy themselves and to feel part of the family. Many of the customers became family friends, and seeing Uncle Gary and I there, knowing that it was our home, made the restaurant more intimate.

"When Mamma was a little girl, I lived in a villa. It was Grandpa's restaurant, La Villa, located at the southwest city limits, far from the Italian community, where his first two restaurants had been. An Italian villa is a sizeable country house with a lot of land. In fact, Grandpa Gene's restaurant was a large, white house on three acres of land, with a barn and a chicken coop. We lived above the restaurant for many years. Grandma cooked dinner every night for Uncle Gary and me: meat and vegetables. We ate in the restaurant dining room, before it got busy. Ugh. I knew that if I could escape to the kitchen, my father would save me from another meat and vegetable dinner. Only his spaghetti, rigatoni, penne, and ravioli, could satisfy my hunger.

"He patted my head and said, 'Aspetta, bambina. Wait until the next customer come and when I cook for them, I'm a gonna put a little bit extra in the pot for you.'

"You see, Grandpa Gene and I had a very special bonding we called the 'spaghetti tie.' Grandpa discovered this when I was three years old while we were on vacation in Idaho. In those days, in the mid-1950s, we would drive to the nearby States, for a holiday. When we stopped for the day, Grandpa would see if there was an Italian restaurant nearby. When he found one, he ordered spaghetti. It arrived and he dished it out. We tasted it. Grandpa waited.

"'You call this spaghetti!' I wailed.

"Grandpa scooped me into his arms and cried, '*Che piccolina!* That's a my baby, she knows a good spaghetti.'

"From that day on, whenever I asked Grandpa for spaghetti, he made it for me. You see Grandpa's idea was to create the best of Italy, as he remembered it. He introduced many new foods to Calgarians: breadsticks, veal scaloppini, chicken cacciatore, ravioli, and pizza. He wanted the customers to enjoy the food and each other. He added a large dance floor so that diners could dance to the jukebox. Grandma greeted customers at the door. Grandpa would go to the dining room for little visits, answering questions, suggesting different items, telling stories, inquiring about their families. If he had time, he would sit down for coffee and a chat. Italian friends often called ahead to request their favourites. They usually sat in a more secluded spot. Grandpa would bring the food himself and eat with them. They spoke in dialect.

Sometimes Jewish friends would call days ahead if they required foods prepared in a special way. Grandpa insisted on an open kitchen so diners could see him cook. They felt that they were at a friend's house.

"Sundays were special. People, who had dined and danced at La Villa on Friday or Saturday night returned on Sunday with the children and the grandparents to enjoy a family dinner. The children often played together around the juke box and the customers mingled. You see, La Villa was really a *piazza*, a public meeting space, where Italians, Jews, Americans, Catholics, Protestants, oil executives, business and professional people, labourers, politicians, entertainers, professional hockey players, boxers, and tourists all came together. Grandpa and Grandma were there to welcome them all, to fulfill requests for extra helpings or bags of breadsticks to take home to the children.

"The Calgary Stampeders football players often ate at La Villa. I recall one evening when they came in after a game. Grandpa was busy cooking when a customer rushed into the kitchen and demanded, 'You must ask those *black* players to leave. I will not eat in the same place with them. Either they go or I go!'

"Grandpa Gene put down his pot and said, 'Tell a me, you have a season tickets to the football games, yes? Well, you're a very lucky! Tonight, you a gonna eat with them too! Your dinner's ready. Come, I'll take it to your table.' The customer sat down and ate.

"Grandpa thought of customers as guests in his house. He went out of his way to make them feel comfortable. It was *his* home though. He made the rules and saw that they were followed."

⁓

When Rafaela was five years old I enrolled her in a summer day camp. Picking her up one afternoon, all she could talk about was the fun she had had on a group picnic. That night, I told her, "When Mamma was a little girl, we went on family picnics to Banff. An Italian family picnic is a lot of fun. Loads of relatives came and we brought a big pot to cook the spaghetti.

"Grandpa Gene had a swimming rule just for picnics. 'No desserts after eating! This a way we swim sooner, after *secondo*, and not after *dolci*.'

"We drove in two cars: Auntie Gisetta, Grandpa's older sister, and her daughter Connie with us, and cousin Jean and her husband Jack with their three daughters in the other.

"Picnics were always at the same grounds, by the river. We knew the routine: the kids ran to get the three picnic tables nearest to the shelter with the stove while the adults unloaded the food and dishes. Grandpa Gene found the large pot, filled it with water from the little tap outside the shelter, and put it on stove to boil. He and Auntie would then sit and talk in dialect, *la lingua segreta*, about the family, the local Italian community in Calgary, and news from their hometown. Soon enough, the boiling water would call them to action. We set the tables with plastic tablecloths and old mismatched dishes, glasses, and silverware."

"Did other people think it was strange that our family was cooking pasta in the middle of a park?" asked Rafi.

"If they did, Grandpa just shrugged his shoulders, puzzled that anyone would care what we ate. He would smile and call '*Mangiamo!*' and that was that.

"We sat down, said grace, and the spaghetti was served. It was *primo*, the first course. *Secondo* was hamburgers, hot dogs, and salad made from the best of Auntie's garden.

"When we finished eating, Grandpa looked at his watch. 'In an hour we can go swimming, but remember, no *dolci*, no dessert, justa watermelon.' We grabbed pieces of bright red, juicy fruit and waited for swim time."

Rafaela loved to celebrate Christmas and also Hanukkah with her father's relatives. Once she started school, she began to realize that not all families were like hers. By the time she was seven, she was questioning why religions were different. At eight, she wanted to know the relationship between religion and being a good person. She recalled a story that I had told many years earlier.

"When Mamma was a little girl, I ate and danced with nuns and priests. I don't mean just my cousin, Father Mageste. Grandpa was generous; he loved to cook for others. After all, Grandpa would remind us that being devoted to God didn't mean giving up Italian food. Both Uncle Gary and I went to Sacred Heart School; he was in Grade 9 and I just started Grade 1. There was no bus service near La Villa, so Grandpa drove us home after school. This is how he met our teachers, the Ursuline nuns. Before long, he had invited himself to their convent to cook a special Italian dinner. At the time, there were about twenty nuns living there.

"He arrived with several boxes and was soon busy at work. The tables were set with a white linen tablecloth and candles.

"'Here, put a my special glasses on the table,' he requested.

"After grace, Grandpa described the various courses they would be eating that evening and disappeared into the kitchen. He returned with the antipasto and with wine. The nuns were surprised; they didn't drink. But Grandpa said, '*Gesù beveva vino!* If it was a good enough for Jesus, it's a good enough for you. *Salute!*' Watching Mother Superior lift her glass and sip, the nuns took their cue and toasted. Smiles rippled across their faces and they began to eat. By the second course they were ready for a refill. After dinner they adjourned to the music room. Grandpa cleaned up the kitchen, enjoying choruses from a Rosetti opera drifting in from the other room.

"After this, our teachers sometimes came to La Villa for an early dinner. Dressed in long black habits that covered their shoes, they seemed to float to the table, creatures from another era. Grandma seated them and asked what they wished to drink.

"'What we had at the convent would be nice.'

"After a few sips of wine, their bodies relaxed and they were like other customers, chatting and enjoying good food."

Rafaela asked, "Did Grandpa go to church?"

"Yes, when he lived in the Italian neighbourhood. It was near his restaurant. He and Grandma got married there and that's where Uncle Gary and I were baptized. Grandpa Gene supported the church by doing good works for the priests and the nuns. Remember that La Villa was at the city limits. In time, a new parish, Holy

Name, was established nearby. After church one Sunday, Grandpa invited the priests to the restaurant for dinner with our family. They spoke about how difficult it was to start a new parish and how little money they had.

"Grandpa wanted to help them so he started the annual Holy Name Spaghetti Dinner, a fundraiser for the church. It was on a Monday, the day the restaurant normally closed. It was announced in church and hundreds of people came, paying five dollars each to enjoy spaghetti and meatballs, salad, and ice cream. He raised thousands of dollars for the parish over the years.

"A dear friend of Grandpa's was a Franciscan priest, Father Tim. Sometimes Grandpa cooked at the Franciscan Retreat House but Father Tim also ate at La Villa often and was invited to festivities for special customers and friends. At La Villa, Father Tim met and became friends with a Calgary football player named Don. Unfortunately, Don had a very serious ski accident, which kept him in a hospital bed for nearly a year. Father Tim tended to his spirit and Grandpa nourished his body, sending Italian food to the hospital by taxi. They didn't give up. Don eventually recovered and was able to walk again.

"Some months after opening the restaurant, an exhausted Grandma said that she had worked enough that day.

"Grandpa said, 'Martha, do you wanna work hard like a this when you are old?'

"She shook her head.

"'Then a let's work hard now.'

"And so they worked their way into Calgary's history."

Those Nutty Days of Disco

NETTA RONDINELLI

Anabelle wasn't allowed to wear jeans. My father didn't think they would flatter her figure. My mother bought her dresses that were labelled *grande* — the shapeless kind that were made for older ladies. My sister wanted jeans so badly she stole a pair from our neighbour, Susan. Susan had hung her laundry on our clothesline because she had a lot. Susan's daughter and I got a real kick of seeing our matching rainbow-coloured underwear adorned with the days of the week hanging together on the line.

My sister Anabelle hardly went outside. Her skin was paper white. Papa said her skin was like porcelain and that when she was little she looked like a china doll. If she hadn't been so fat, she might have resembled Snow White. After my nonna arrived from Italy and moved in with us, she changed that. She fed Anabelle *zabaglione* for breakfast every day — hardly a balanced breakfast. By the time Anabelle was thirteen, she was wearing mamma's clothes. My parents wouldn't let her walk around the block, for fear that something would happen to her. After my parents realized how unhealthy *zabaglione* was, we were relegated to eating smelly cereal with hot milk. My younger sister, Louise, preferred to eat her cereal with a thin skin of boiled milk on top.

"Your sister is even afraid of the furnace. Once we found her crying because she thought there was a monster in the furnace. Your sister's a scaredy-cat," Papa chuckled.

Anabelle escaped my parents by secluding herself in a sanctuary of romance novels, finishing them as quickly as she gobbled her chocolate bars. I hardly ever saw her and when I did we fought. Once when I was play-fighting with Anabelle, I stuck a pin in her to see if she'd pop like a balloon. I thought she was going to kill me, but she just called me an f'n idiot and went back to her bedroom.

When Papa heard that Anabelle had stolen Susan's jeans, he went on a rampage. Susan went to pick up her laundry and saw there was a gap where her new, heart-shaped pocket jeans had once hung. There was only one explanation: Anabelle.

I didn't see the point in stealing the jeans; it wasn't as if they were going to fit her. When we were bad, Mamma used to taunt us with a ridiculous Italian phrase, which roughly translated means, "I wish you were a piece of cheese, at least I could eat you." Anabelle should have stolen her favourite food over the jeans with the heart-shaped pockets; at least she could have eaten it and got rid of the evidence.

I followed Papa into Anabelle's room and shuddered when he lifted her orange comforter. An empty jar of Nutella — no sign of a spoon. Under no circumstances were we allowed to eat in our bedrooms, only *sporcacionas* did that. Dirty girls. Our bedrooms were only for sleeping; we didn't even do homework or play there with our friends.

"Unbelievable, your sister says she's dieting and I find this!" Papa exclaimed.

From under the bed, Papa pulled out rumpled jeans, candy wrappers, dirty socks, and a charcoal sweater.

"She has no shame. Stealing from strangers and now my sweater." Papa said. "I'm taking her out of that goddamn school and sending her somewhere strict with priests and nuns. Then she'll see." Mamma watched from a distance and shook her head.

"What a *sporcaciona* your sister is. I didn't teach her to be dirty. How did she become this way?" Mamma cried. Thank God Mamma didn't check under my bed. She would have discovered that she had another *sporcaciona* in the house.

My sister had a lot of *mangiacake* friends whom Papa didn't like, so she decided to blame the missing items on one of them, a skinny girl named Kim, who shared a locker with Anabelle. She was the one who had stolen Anabelle's lunches and nearly incited a riot.

As for the Nutella, instead of confronting Anabelle directly, Papa left a spoon and jar of the hazelnut spread on the bathroom counter and waited for her. I didn't think that was very fair, it was the last jar of our beloved Nutella and it would take a full week before Mamma would replace it. Papa wanted to show us that he knew everything we were up to. If he wasn't such a know-it-all, Anabelle wouldn't have to be so sneaky-sneaky.

My sister must have had her chocolate radar on because she didn't give Papa the satisfaction of walking into the bathroom. She pushed me out of her way and muttered under her breath. "Get out of my face, you f'n idiot!" slamming her bedroom door behind her. In a matter of minutes, "Ring My Bell" was blasting in the background. She thought that I had squealed. The floorboards squeaked.

"If she isn't careful, Papa will show her," Mamma cautioned.

Everyone in our family liked to dance, even Mamma. At weddings, she would waken from the heaviness of an eight-course meal to dance her favourite tarantella. She looked like a school girl, dancing with her sisters and hopping about. I preferred disco. So did Anabelle. I think my sister wanted to be like Tony Manero from *Saturday Night Fever*, especially when he looked at himself in the mirror. Anabelle thought she was so cool.

∼

One fall day my cousins Gio and Angelica visited. We had nothing to do. There were no grasshoppers to torture and we'd already gotten into trouble for throwing rocks at a neighbour's dog — my Barbies were next. We didn't trust each other enough to play hide and seek. Whenever

Louise was "it," we'd leave her counting at her post and start an entirely new game. Suddenly, we heard disco music blaring from my basement. We trampled across my father's flowerbeds and pressed our faces against the basement window. Inside, Anabelle was swinging her hips, her lips puckered in a disco pout. I was kind of impressed until she lost her balance and fell. That was it; we couldn't control our laughter. Anabelle looked up and saw us spying on her.

"Fuck off," she screamed, holding her ankle in pain. Aunts, uncles, and cousins came to see what all the fuss was about. My father, the "know-it-all," and my grandmother, "hawk-eyes" were first on the scene.

"Look at you! I heard you fall from next door. You don't know how to do these gymnastics. There are books in the library that tell you how to stretch!" my father said.

My grandmother's eyes were fixed on Anabelle's bulging ankle. "Show me where it hurts. I don't think it's broken. Stay put." My grandmother quickly returned with a tub of lard and her bifocals.

"Ugh, that lard is not touching me!" cried Anabelle.

My cousins and I exchanged glances. Lard for the lard ass.

~

Papa had rules when it came to boys. They were simply out of the question unless my father hand-picked them. He had attempted to set Anabelle up with our *paesan's* son Marcello. Anabelle didn't like him because he was too dark and hairy and I think she already had her eyes on someone else — a boy she had met on her own. I learned this from eavesdropping on her phone conversations. I'd unscrew the receiver so she couldn't hear me breathing.

"He looks like Tom Selleck," Anabelle giggled. "I think he digs me too. He told his friend that if I was skinny, he'd go out with me."

On the phone she called him by his code name, "Sally," when my parents were in the room. If papa answered, "Sally" would hang up. One day Papa became suspicious and cornered me.

"Your sister thinks I'm stupid. You think I don't know about this boy?"

I shrugged my shoulders. I didn't think I was going to get out of this one, and I was right.

"Don't even try lying to me," he said. "I know everything that happens in this house."

I told him enough to satisfy his curiosity, but didn't tell him about the phone calls. If Papa found out, he'd take away my phone privileges, too.

From then on, Papa watched Anabelle's every move. Rainy days made this easier because he worked in construction and got to stay home on those days. Mamma also liked rainy days. Every night I had to call the weather number and listen for the forecast. On this particular day, there was an 80 per cent chance of rain. This meant Papa would probably pick my mother up from work after doing some errands.

Anabelle wasn't thinking; she skipped school on a rainy afternoon. Papa was at the mall getting groceries when he saw her.

"That Anabelle has no brains. She thinks that I don't know anything. I know what she does before she does it," Papa boasted.

He hadn't let on he'd seen her and returned home to vacuum the whole house. He was up to something, I just didn't know what. From the corner of my eye I could see a jar of Nutella, a spoon in the bathroom.

"Don't touch that. It's for your sister!" Papa shouted. I would never eat Nutella again.

Papa sat in his favourite reclining chair, read the Italian newspaper and waited. When Anabelle walked in he asked, "How did you like the mall?"

She whimpered a bit, took off her glasses, wiped them with the edge of her sleeve and headed up to her bedroom.

Papa never gave Anabelle the trouble he gave me.

Anabelle continued to see "Sally." He had a moustache. It grossed me out even thinking about her kissing him. I knew she did because she would come home from school with a rash on her chin. Thankfully, Papa didn't notice.

That summer, Anabelle spent less time in her bedroom and more time in our basement. The basement was fully equipped to satisfy all our disco needs. The hi-fi stereo system was encased in a faux wooden bar. A screen with multi-coloured lights flashed to the beat of the music, even to the beat of my mother's favourite Calabrese tarantella. When it was disco time, I drew the blinds, my cousin Angelica stuffed cushions in sunlit crevices to darken the room, and Anabelle lined up the eight tracks.

We danced to Anabelle's favourite tune, "Ring My Bell." Before the music played, she'd prepare by sucking in her cheeks and staring at herself in the mirror. We got behind her and followed my sister across the coarse orange rug.

She led us in a string of dance moves, bouncing, side-stepping, pointing up and down. One afternoon, her powder-blue gabardine pants tore during a particularly taxing move. She tip-toed backwards trying to hide the huge tear along the seam. No one laughed. Jeans would have been a sturdier choice, stolen or not.

~

None of this deterred my sister from dancing: in fact, she continued dancing even in front of my family at my aunt's wedding. The dance floor was otherwise deserted because someone had died that week, and out of respect, people chose not to dance.

We hadn't seen Anabelle for the better part of the evening, but when the music began Anabelle appeared from nowhere, shimmying her way to the centre of the dance floor. Mamma and her sisters turned their chairs so they could have a better view.

Anabelle was acting "big" in front of a moustached usher, who looked more like Lurch than Tom Selleck. I, however, could see right through her phony act. If he only knew that she had a jar of Nutella under her bed.

Italian By a Nose

VALERIE SOVRAN MITCHELL

When I was a teenager growing up in the '60s in my hometown of Trail, British Columbia, I said a prayer each night asking to look like Sharon Johnson. Reflecting now on that nightly appeal, I realize what an impossible challenge I was issuing. You see, Sharon had long, fine, silver-blond hair with a gentle wave that fell softly across her shoulders. Her crystal-blue eyes were positioned just the right distance from the feature I envied most — a perfect little upturned nose.

I, on the other hand, have facial features that spring from the unadulterated Italian gene pools of my Abruzzese mother and my Friulano father — thick, dark hair that bends and curls in the presence of the slightest mist, deep brown eyes that are framed by circles when I don't get enough sleep, and (how I used to cringe at the adjective) a Roman nose. Up until the age of 11 or 12, I lived happily in this body, concerned with it only to tend to cuts and bruises from playground spills or broken bones from track meets and softball games. If I occasionally compared my features to those of others, it was an easy and comfortable comparison. My role models were Italian neighbourhood friends and family. I looked like my world and my world looked like me.

Then, just as we entered the hormonal turbulence of adolescence, my small group of childhood friends and I moved on to the city-wide secondary school, where we were swept up in a sea of new faces. Suddenly, my world didn't look so much like me. In fact, all I could see was a flotilla of differences and, somehow, I was on the wrong boat.

I tormented myself with the images of perfect teenage girls (who surely must have been related to Sharon

Johnson) in *Seventeen* magazine. I contemplated my impossibly shaped and nasally upturned Barbie doll (albeit one of the few models with curly brown hair, a tribute to my parents who carefully selected the closest Mediterranean-featured prototype) and I despaired. What choice did I have? I ironed the kinks from my long mane, I avoided displaying my profile in pictures, and yes, I occasionally lay in bed at night gently pushing up on the tip of my nose in the hope that it might be trained to change direction with a little encouragement.

Don't get me wrong. I had no desire to renounce my Italian heritage. Not for a second. I loved being Italian and growing up in an Italian family. Even at an age when I was still wobbly on sturdy little brown legs, I knew I had roots that reached far beyond my circumscribed world. My father transported us — my older sister, my younger brother, and me — with stories about "the old country," stories about raising silkworms, crushing the grapes, tasting the *grappa*. I used to imagine him with his big dark eyes and his thick black hair, eagerly scooping up his *baccala* with a wedge of polenta. I was there with him when he rode in the big hay-filled cart. His hometown of San Martino al Tagliamento became my Narnia.

My mother delighted us with stories about growing up in the Gulch, the neighbourhood in Trail where many

Italian immigrants made their first home in Canada and which, at its peak, was a hearty minestrone of different Italian dialects and traditions. Interspersed among the modest houses sat the *bocce* pit, the Catholic Church, the soda fountain, the tailor, the bakery, and the beer parlour — each the setting of many stories, some reaching legendary proportions in their retelling. We pictured young Eleanor, her thick dark hair pinned back to reveal her at once serious and shyly playful countenance, watching for Papa to come home from work at the smelter that loomed above the Gulch.

I had the good fortune, too, of growing up near both sets of grandparents; each had emigrated to Canada in their 20s and settled in Trail to raise their young families. Nonna Linda and Nonno Lino Sovran, my father's Friulano parents, lived "up the hill"; Nonna Sofia and Papa Vincenzo Poscente, my mother's Abruzzese parents, lived "down the Gulch." Both were within walking distance of our house. My sister Lorraine and I (and eventually our little brother, Linne) spent countless hours basking in their adoring love, devouring wonderful food, and pursuing our bi-regional Italian apprenticeship.

So, how could I embrace everything about growing up Italian except my Mediterranean looks? How could I have passion for polenta but not pride in my proboscis?

Revel in my Italian roots but curse my coarse, dark curls? In the self-absorbed world of an adolescent, comparison with my peers — at school or in movies and magazines — was the only thing that mattered when it came to appearance. The fact that I thought my mother pretty and my father handsome did not seem dissonant with my view of how I stacked up. They were adults; I was a teenager.

If I had applied my otherwise inquiring mind to the matter, I might have searched out and found solace in the wisdom of Gertrude Stein — "a nose is a nose is a nose" — or considered the female form celebrated in the works of da Vinci or Michaelangelo, or even recognized a parallel between my teenage penchant for self-deprecation and that of most of my peers.

But this is the rational analysis of a 53-year-old woman looking back on the thoughts of a 15-year-old and finding them faulty. At the time, it all made complete, if dispiriting, sense to me. Fortunately, I inherited my mother's tenacity and my father's pragmatism. I did what I could to discipline my obstinate curls, I always looked directly into a camera lens, I said my nightly secret prayer — and I got on with things. I decided that I might not be able to change the direction of my nose, but I could set the direction of my life.

Over time, as most adolescent agonies do, my angst diminished and concerns about appearance competed with concerns about studies, careers, and futures. There was too much else to think about to spend time worrying about something I couldn't change. And frankly, I think I finally tired of living with the cognitive dissonance of loving my Italian heritage but lamenting my Latin looks.

The seed of self-acceptance was finally planted when I moved from my small hometown to a big city university. Suddenly, the mythical standard of perfect appearance that I had concocted as a teenager evaporated in the cosmopolitan diversity of the student body and the variety of fashion norms of the early '70s. The American rock musical *Hair* had by then given voice to a new generation's rejection of everything from pollution to sexual repression, and questioned prevailing standards that shackled individualism and personal expression. The popular writings of Kahlil Gibran ("Say not 'I have found *the* truth' but rather 'I have found *a* truth'") took over from the vacuous advice offered up in teen magazines. The new wisdom could be summarized in two words: "Anything goes."

One of my favourite photographs of those early, heady days provides proof of my budding self-acceptance. My husband and I discovered each other in our early 20s. I loved everything about him and he loved everything about me — from head to heart and nose to toes. The picture is of the two of us in a grinning embrace — our faces both in profile.

Then there was a pivotal experience with a new hairdresser when we moved to Victoria. I had stopped staring into camera lenses by then, but I was still going to great lengths to straighten my hair. I curled it with enormous soup cans each night and fashioned various head coverings to serve as vapour barriers when I went outside into the wet west coast air. Examining my heat-and-curler-damaged mane on my first visit to his salon, Darren looked up at me in the mirror with a concerned expression and asked quizzically: "Why are you fighting your curls?" I paused, considered, and then asked myself the same question. Why indeed? I authorized him to unleash his shears and free my Italian curls from years of captivity.

My husband and I also made the customary pre-children pilgrimage to Europe to discover our roots. When we stepped off the train in Rome, everywhere I looked, there were thick wavy tresses framing olive-skinned faces and noses of all sizes — some arcing gently, some prominently. "Roman" nose took on a whole new meaning. Just as I did when I was a child in the bosom of my family and my little circle of Italian friends, I felt a deep sense of belonging.

But it wasn't until the arrival of our children, first one daughter, then a second four years later, that self-acceptance fully blossomed. When they were babies, Lindsay, and then Ali, loved to play the game of *"niso naso."* I would lay them on their backs on a blanket and get down on my knees with my face above theirs. Their tiny feet would start kicking in glee as they reached up with small, eager hands and took a fistful of my hair in each one, pulling my head down until our noses touched. That was my cue to nuzzle gently from side to side and sing *"niso naso."*

Lindsay and Ali gurgled with unbridled delight, their cheeks tickled by my thick curls as the tips of their noses caressed mine.

Once a Catholic

LUCIANA RICCIUTELLI

Confession was the worst. I hated it. I went to a Catholic elementary school and on the first Friday of every month mass was held in the gymnasium. Everyone was expected to attend, which meant everyone had to go to confession on Wednesday. *That* meant you had to be good all night Wednesday, all day Thursday, and all morning Friday. It was next to impossible. But refusing to take holy communion was more impossible — everyone would know you had sinned in the last 48 hours.

On Wednesdays we filed down the hallway leading to the room where the priest was hearing confession. We weren't allowed to talk in line because we were supposed to be gravely contemplating the error of our ways. Being grave at the age of seven (that's when the indoctrination begins) wasn't easy. Huddling together, clammy hands clasped tightly in prayer, we would try very hard to look remorseful — especially when the teacher walked by.

My mother used to tell me that God saw everything, and I mean *everything*, I did. She used to say it with a look that implied that He would then tell *her* everything. I imagined an angry and menacing God frowning down upon me, then my mother chasing me with a broom (or a shoe, or a wooden spoon) around the kitchen table, then kneeling in front of a priest dressed in long flowing black robes, thick fingers clutching an oversized black rosary, as he waited impatiently to hear my confession.

I was, needless to say, very intimidated. "Bless me father for I have sinned . . ." I would mutter under my breath, trying to get the whole thing over with as soon as possible. My heart beat wildly, pulsating through my sweater. I clasped my hands piously against my chest to keep it in place. Beads of perspiration accumulated on my trembling upper lip. Kneeling at the priest's feet, I knew the only thing that could save me was keeping my eyes stubbornly fixed on the scuff marks on his big black shoes.

It was time to recite my litany of sins. Now, I ask you, how many things can a seven-year-old do wrong? Too young to know any better, I mumbled that I didn't really think I *had* any sins to confess. This was not a good idea.

"My child, no one, but no one, is perfect! You must have done something wrong!" exclaimed the priest.

Face hot, eyes welling with tears, I admitted that I disobeyed my mother once or twice; I fought with my brother more than once; and I told a lie here and there. That was my first lesson: no one is ever free from sin.

Later, I learned it was much easier to make things up. It never crossed my mind to worry about the fact that I was lying. Eventually, I didn't have to worry about making things up at all because I had plenty of examples from my everyday life. As long as I was "heartily sorry" for my sins, and I did my penance with sincere remorse, my soul would be clear. What I worried about was how to be "sincerely" remorseful. As I cited my penance — usually one Our Father, three Hail Marys, and a Glory Be — I would catch myself drifting off into a terrific daydream somewhere in the middle of the whole thing. Then, certain I had been less than sincere, I would have to start all over again. Sometimes it would take me hours. As I got older, the penance increased. So did the day-dreaming. After all, no one is perfect, and you're likely doing something wrong almost all the time. Even *thinking* about doing something wrong is a sin. You can't win.

Guilt is what makes the Catholic world go round. Without guilt, the whole structure of the Catholic religion would collapse. It is, in fact, the only religion in which an infant is born with sin, the original sin of Adam and Eve. Thus the need for baptism. If you were un-fortunate enough to die without having been baptized, you were condemned to limbo, a place where you had to stay for all eternity without a prayer in the world of ever getting to heaven!

It is important to remember that original sin was all Eve's fault. She succumbed to temptation by desiring knowledge and thus falling prey to seductive Satan. Then, as if that wasn't bad enough, she enticed the pure and noble Adam, created in the image of God himself, into her web of deceit. The fall of mankind therefore rests on woman's depraved shoulders. As punishment, she was condemned to a life of eternal subjugation to her lord and master — man.

My second lesson: women are evil and purity (read

chastity) is their only salvation. Mandatory virginity is considered the only way of ensuring a measure of control over women's "inherent" wantonness, something that can only lead to no good. We are told to bear our husband's children but to take no pleasure in their conception. In Sicily, you can still find women's nightshirts hand embroidered, just above the breasts, with the following quotation: *Non lo fo per piacer mio, ma lo fo per piacer di dio* ("I do not do it for my pleasure, but for the pleasure of God"). Sound like fun?

It was all part of God's, and my mother's, great plan. My future husband, whenever he happened along, would test me several times, trying to entice me into having sex with him before marriage. I was not to be fooled. For, should I succumb, not only would he promptly leave me, never to be heard of again, but I would be *rovinata* (ruined), unable to raise my eyes to a man from that moment forward. Sex — the mere suggestion of which was enough to inspire shudders of abject horror in any Italian mother — included kissing, petting, and slow dancing!

I was in Grade 5 the first time I kissed a boy. I didn't like him that much, but I was pleased to *finally* have a boyfriend after years of being too pudgy or too bookish. I developed breasts and *voilà* there he was! Breasts can do that for a girl. I think my mother knew that too, so this was about the time that our sex talks began. Although this very wet and sloppy kiss on the cheek in the middle of the park behind our house was nothing to brag about, suddenly, all the stories about girls who let guys kiss them in the park came back to me. I turned around and ran home as fast as I could; the guilt had kicked in. Oh my God! I had gone and done it. That's it, I was ruined, spoiled goods, finished. I would never be able to look a man in the face again. God would never forgive me and neither would my mother!

After I recovered from the shame of my transgression, I recorded the entire event in my diary, at the best of times half fact and half romantic fiction. Some days later, upon returning home from school after a leisurely walk in the park with the newly acquired boyfriend, I entered the house to face a raging mother who unleashed an array of flying objects and screeched, "*Putana!* Whore!" My diary, once hidden under my mattress, was on my dresser open to the offending page. The next day at school I told my boyfriend I could never walk home with him again. I never kept a diary again either.

By Grade 7 I had managed to quash the guilt my curiosity about sex inevitably gave rise to. I, at last, had a real boyfriend who I was crazy about. He had failed three times and was the oldest boy in school. He drove a hot car, had long hair, and sported the first single earring. And, he respected me, that is, he didn't "test" me (by then, I was firmly convinced kissing didn't count). When my teacher caught us walking up the stairs together doing the forbidden — holding hands — she asked me to stay after class. "Only sluts behave that way," she explained calmly in the face of tears and a sputtering plea for the trivial nature of our offence. Holding hands, she insisted, could only lead to worse. "Good" girls did not allow themselves to be touched. Period. The teacher, on the other hand, came to school dressed in mini skirts with nothing but her pantyhose between her thighs and the stares of 30 students as she bent over a desk to help with school work, giving the entire class an unrestricted view. Ah, the hypocrisy.

In high school, the preoccupation with sex became an even greater concern. I went to an all-girls Catholic high school and the nuns that taught there knew what we could get up to. The skirts of our uniforms had to be no more than four inches above our knees, lest we provoke male attention. Every month we were subjected to an inspection. All the girls had to kneel in a row while the nuns measured the distance between the hem of our skirt and our knees. Anything over four inches meant you had to go home and redo the hem (which took forever because the skirt was pleated) and you were condemned to detention for a week. If you were caught outside school grounds with your skirt hoisted up to mid-thigh, as was the common practice, you had detention for a month. If you were caught speaking to the boys of the pagan public high school next door, execution was recommended.

We were to be kept from losing our virginity, at all costs. And, if it did somehow get lost, the guilt would be unbearable. I know girls who married the first guy they slept with because they were convinced no one else would have them. As for me, I was brazen. I didn't like to be told what to do. A healthy dose of cynicism didn't hurt either.

When I finally did it, to my dismay the big event wasn't big at all, and it certainly didn't live up to my daydreams. To top it all off, the gentleman involved, from an older generation, paused to comment with undisguised regret that, in keeping with Italian tradition, he had hoped to carry the proof of my deflowering on the perfectly folded white handkerchief he pulled out of his pocket. Dumbfounded, I rose to go to the bathroom. And there, what should I see floating unabashedly in the toilet but the missing proof of my innocence. I looked at it for some time. I had always wondered what it looked like. I considered offering it to him in my defence. I must have been in there for quite some time because he eventually knocked on the door.

"What's the matter?" he asked.

"Nothing," I replied, flushing my innocence unceremoniously down the toilet.

It wasn't until recently that I really understood the dilemma that women face in the Catholic church. The most revered woman for a Catholic is the Virgin Mary, who is both a mother and a virgin, something that no woman can ever hope to be. As I said, you can't win. And, although the Virgin Mary holds a privileged position, she really has no power at all. Jesus, we were taught, answered your prayers and He could not refuse his mother anything, so Mary was helpful too, but the implication was that she, personally, couldn't grant you a thing. That was exclusively male domain. This troubled me, got me to thinking, to asking questions that begged more questions. I'm still looking for the answers. Yet, as they say, once a Catholic, always a Catholic, and, in the back of my mind, I think He'll get me for this. And if He doesn't, my mother will.

Apologia for Singledom

JENNIFER FEBBRARO

Every time I go home to Sault Ste. Marie, I revisit the "make-out" landmarks scattered across the city that recall my romantic history. The now rotting benches of Penhorwood Park's tennis courts, the blue tin portables behind Mount St. Joseph's girls' school, discreet corners of the bungalow-laden, P-named streets known as the P-patch, the back lot of the Algoma Art Gallery facing the

St. Mary's river, and the desolate locks that serve as gateway to our twin city in Michigan — taken together these industrial backdrops became the sacred settings for the most romantic moments of my life. Too bad they all took place before the age of 17.

I had boyfriends (read: potential husbands) from the ages of 6 to 27, but then, just when I was expected to achieve marital bliss, the sea of candidates dried up. Was it mere coincidence, karma, or my unconscious resistance to doing what was expected that rendered me chronically single from that point on? After all, I lived in Toronto where there were plenty of other single people roaming the streets and no one seemed to take notice or offence at my status. As long as I stayed clear of the 'burbs and attended only a few couple-only parties, I was safe from having to explain whether I was post-breakup, in-between boyfriends, at the crush stage, or simply single "by my own hand."

I was not alone in my suffering. The unmarried inevitably endure a social cramp under the vice-grip that is compulsory couplehood. However, the plight of the single girl is significantly more tragic if she is a member of an Italian family. It really wasn't until I went home to the Soo, where my father's family immigrated in 1950, that I became hyper-aware of my oddity. There I was, a lone unicorn walking the plank while all the other animals boarded the ark two by two. I was greeted by a host of cloying endearments: "You will meet someone soon. Your 'time' has not yet come. Everything will work out as it should. We will keep you in our prayers." I was assured I was pretty while my cheeks were twisted like radio dials — singledom was marring me for life.

Luckily my parents didn't pressure me to marry. My mother was not Italian, but of Mennonite and British descent, which made for odd hybrids like Yorkshire pudding and biscotti, mincemeat pies and Calabrese frittata, and tea in espresso cups. Genetically, I may have only been 50 per cent Italian, but it felt like a whole lot more. We only saw my mother's relatives on brief stints at holidays, as they visited us from Ottawa, from Vancouver, from Fort McMurray, whereas we were in almost constant contact with the Italian side of the family, all of whom lived within a couple miles of each other in the Soo.

It's no wonder my mother felt like a stranger in a strange land. When my father first brought her home to meet his family, they were all in the basement decapitating chickens. There they were swinging poultry by their claws, gobbling heads knocking against metal posts, plucked feathers clouding the air. It was enough to send my mother screaming up the stairs to the guest bedroom (complete with mounted crucifix and rosary), where she proclaimed all of them barbarians and prayed to her Anglican God for salvation.

My mother's choice to settle in Sault Ste. Marie was not a mistake, but it was difficult. However, her choice did offer us cultural alternatives and introduced variety denied to my cousins born of two Italian parents. Thanks to my mother, I learned that it was not required décor to have Leonardo da Vinci's "Last Supper" painting hanging in your kitchen. My mother's choice of robin's egg blue cupboards and her purchase of original, rather than wholesale artwork, broke with Italian tradition. We didn't have a second kitchen in our basement or a dining room with plastic-encased furniture. My mother was utilitarian in her taste, but also stylish. There was no tip-toeing around bric-a-brac in glass cases in our house.

My sisters and I grew up under the "If you're happy, we're happy" rule of parenting. Somehow this quest for the Authentic, Happy Self led to the post-modern condition that is graduate school. Here, I found myself lecturing on the semantics of truth, identity politics, and the philosophical dimensions of "the good life." Who knew that when I'd won that city-wide oral competition in '86, a presentation punctuated with quotes from *The*

Deserata and Burger King's "Where's the Beef?" campaign and ominously titled *Who Am I?*, that I'd be rewriting the same speech for the next 20 years?

My parents wanted me to "fulfill my potential" while the culture-at-large expected me to marry a good Italian boy, but somehow these two choices, which on the surface appear to overlap, became polar opposites in my mind. Perhaps this occurred in response to disheartening dinner conversations in which my two physician parents regaled us with tales of life's fickle twists: men falling into pits of molten steel, children mysteriously born with missing limbs, heroin overdoses. We listened to the tales of sexual assault and abuse with the morbid curiosity of girls at a slumber party hearing a ghost story. Between the main course and dessert we'd learn the forensic specifics of the rape kit (my mother was the only doctor in the city who could stomach doing it for children) and sometimes there'd be a knock at the door by a woman not unlike those in the stories, begging my mother to pay a house call.

Suffice it to say, these cautionary tales left an impression. The question wasn't so much why wouldn't I want to get married, but why would I? With this evidence of relationships gone wrong on our doorstep, the probability of being victimized by love seemed higher than normal. Catastrophe had been allowed to enter their lives, so why couldn't it enter ours? With a teenager's logic, I rationalized that the best defense against disaster was a refusal to settle.

Of course, there was also the matter of my father. No post-pubescent male ever sufficiently impressed him, no matter how nice or well-intentioned. Nerve-wracked boyfriends endured small talk with my father, flailing for approval despite his bored expression. But it wasn't boredom, it was the pall of experience. My father remembered his own journey as a young boy — from Italy to Halifax (wearing shorts in February so his legs had to be covered with Red Cross blankets) and then by train to Sault Ste. Marie — and he knew the price of naïveté. At four years old, after travelling thousands of miles, my father's first experience of the new country was one of abandonment. His own father left his mother and brothers and sister — none of whom spoke English or were employed at the time — for his brother's wife, but not before insisting that they give my father up for adoption to a related couple who were having infertility problems. Before his wife had the chance to kick him out for suggesting such a thing, his father left.

In contrast to his own father, whose biggest lie was one of omission — he never told his second wife in Montreal that he had four children — my father was a perfect portrait of the honest man protecting his family. When his brothers went to Montreal to make peace with their father, they were introduced as friends of the family. My father knew about nice Italian boys and despite the fact that he was one; he didn't trust them. Nice had nothing on hard-won, cumulative, consistent love, sturdy even through intolerable hardship. This could only be assessed after a lifetime lived one reliable day at a time.

Despite all this, and the melodramatic slamming of doors and smashing of phones that is teenage heartbreak, my father never once said "I told you so." And I gave him plenty of opportunities. In the heartbreak department, I was management. I *was* the Heartbreak Hotel. When I re-enter my old bedroom and look up to that four-by-four foot patch of stucco above my bed, I think of all the would-be movies I projected onto its tired surface. After several hours of semi-hypnosis in lateral position, staring up at the ceiling, I'd imagined its surface had been worn by all the set and costume changes shunted across it: the Grade 7 heartbreaker, also known as Twin #1, when he surprised me with a gold-plated crucifix he'd stolen from the Sault's one and only Station mall. Then there was Twin #2 (Yes, these were identical twins and I dated both of them, chronologically). The most Freudian thing we'd ever done together was bake a cake. But the moment I continued to relive over and over was when we iced our initials — J.F. + E.C. — on top. I also delicately carved them underneath our country-style kitchen table and spray-painted them in black on the basement wall, a few Pink Floyd quotes thrown in to boot. When I went downstairs to the cellar to retrieve some homemade sausage or wine, the shelves shouted: "Mother, do you think they'll drop the bomb?" and "Run like hell."

When these love affairs ended, my father would console me with misattributed words of wisdom: Winston Churchill's "Wisdom is the result of experience, and experience, the result of bad judgment" or Johnny Cash's infamous "You can't always get what you want." If these did not appease the sobbing daughter screaming at him to get the hell out of her room or writing terrible poetry about her 14-year-old fiancé who needed "space," he might try an imitation of Marisa Tomei's "My biological clock is ticking" speech in *My Cousin Vinny* or a scene from a Pink Panther movie. Sometimes I'd act one part, and he'd do the second, in a spontaneous show of father/daughter bonding. Imitating Peter Sellers, he'd say, "Excuse me mister, does your dog bite?" I'd answer, "Why no sir, he doesn't," then snip at his hand. He'd say, "I thought you said your dog doesn't bite?" to which I'd reply, "That sir, is *not* my dog." If that didn't work, my dad would go for the big finish, quoting that great feminist revolutionary Gloria Estefan, who said, "A woman without a man is like a fish without a bicycle."

But those adolescent break-ups were just part of the larger picture, a natural consequence of being a young girl. Everyone, including my parents, always expected another boyfriend to replace the one that had been dumped or who had dumped me. But now I had to select just one — for life.

My parents were in no hurry for this to happen, but my grandmother, sensing her own mortality, was. In the green-and-red brick house my grandfather built, she asked me why I didn't have a boyfriend yet and whatever happened to so-and-so (so-and-so being Alan, an '80s pop musician I dated for several torturous years). Strangely, he was the only boyfriend my grandmother approved of because he was about four feet tall and met her at eye-level. One Christmas I caught Alan and my grandmother gazing approvingly at each other across the candlelit dinner table. She left a lasting impression on him and he still asks about her to this day. I'm thinking of giving him her number. Over delicacies made from pumpkin flowers, oil, batter, and basil (my attempts resembled Tim Hortons' apple fritters, fat dipped in fat with fat sprinkled on top), we talked about "my problem."

Despite having lived in this country for over 50 years, my grandmother still hasn't learned much English, so I could barely understand what she was saying and vice versa. This left us in the precarious position of having to mime most of our dialogue. Try miming Ph.D. Wedding ring is much easier: a simple tap on the appropriate finger of the left hand. My father hadn't passed on the language to his children. He didn't think we'd need it. Or maybe he wanted to protect us from the taunts he suffered as a "D.P.", Displaced Person. At 11, his brother Ernie had been placed in a Grade 3 class and his brother Joe, 15, into Grade 5. It took less than six months before they quit and began working fulltime washing dishes at old Piner's diner on Gore Street. A few years later, Joe left for Toronto to become a semi-successful boxer under the unlikely pseudonym Joey Italiano, taunting the greats like George Chuvalo, but returned to Sault St. Marie to work in the machine shop at Algoma Steel for the next 30 years. Because he was young enough to learn English, my father was able to escape the trap of child labour. He learned to read and write and even built an ECG machine, which won him first place in the high school science contest. Amazingly, he beat future astronaut Roberta Bondar, who came in a distant second.

On the eve of my 31st birthday, my grandmother

contorted her small, frail body before me, squinted painfully as though the blunt fact of my singleness blinded her, then twisted her index finger up to the sky and said with perfect diction, "Your parents want you to get married!"

"We do not!" my mother screamed hysterically from another room.

"Oh come on Na!" I joked. "If you want me to get married, find me somebody."

"Hmmf!" she sighed, then mumbled something in Italian under her breath that sounded like a four-by-four pulling into a gravel driveway.

"She says you're too picky," my father said, interpreting. I chose my battle and decided to fight another day, but I both resented and was amused by my grandmother's feistiness. I leaned into the back of my chair, noting the uselessness of my academic expertise in this situation, and it began to bother me. How could it not? I'd dedicated nearly all my time and money to its pursuit. Why did theory kindly excuse itself when confronted with practice? Why did it make a mad dash for the nearest exit while you pressed the pleats of your best-occasion skirt? Oh, don't worry about that, that's just the last 10 years of my life evacuating the building.

My cousin Lorena is also familiar with these

grandmotherly exchanges. At Christmas or Easter in the Soo, she and I eavesdropped on conversations about fabrics, paint colours, and lawn fertilizers until Lorena paused to mention that she was currently living in Australia. *What?* You mean kangaroos Australia? Koala bears, Olivia Newton John Australia? Did anyone hear what she just said? Nobody seemed to take notice. She had also lived in England, Mexico, Chile, Brazil, and Argentina, but she wasn't married. Being single was a word my Italian relatives couldn't decipher, a code that couldn't be cracked because it existed outside of the language of families and pregnancies, wedding plans and in-laws, houses and swing sets. Not to say that if I discovered the cure for AIDS, everyone wouldn't be very, very proud; but it would only be a matter of seconds before the conversation turned back to the life-and-death issues of insecticide and faux finishes.

Invisibility is the fate of the second-class citizen that is the single girl in the Italian family. Your status is clear — you are third in line. First come couples with children. They've been through it all, orchestrating a wedding, buying a house, raising a child. This entitles them to insights no single person could dream of. It was as though giving birth had endowed them with Socratic powers.

A close second is the as-yet childless couple. And it

goes quite without saying that this couple must be heterosexual. If you are in this situation, count yourself lucky — you're at least on the right track; unless of course, this is your second marriage, and then you've clearly screwed up. Now if you are getting married "later in life," that is after the age of 35, you're a late convert to the life you were born to lead all along. Consult the advice of the married-with-children; this will ensure good standing with the family.

And then there are the singles. To avoid immediate detection, it helps to drag a male around to events who doesn't mind being barraged with questions about his intentions and the degree to which he loves you. Best to choose someone who enjoys gorging on pasta fazouli, but mentally checks out when it comes to conversation. An old high school fling perhaps? Anyone will do. This will give your family the impression you are buying into Darwin's "survival of the fittest" theory: procreate or die. Amazingly, Darwin was not even Italian. But it's Einstein who is on my mind when I am attempting to calculate the measure of a single girl's discomfort: growth rate of pregnant woman's belly x number of baby showers attended = increased likelihood of incarceration in a mental hospital. All the greatest philosophers will tell you there is no light without dark, no good without evil, no life without death. In this world of binaries, the single girl becomes a cardboard cut-out in opposition to the fully formed sculpture of the pregnant woman. How can a family be concerned with half-shadows, when here before them the miracle of life is taking place? No contest.

My cousin Lori is a case in point. Her twin sister Rosa is happily married and pregnant, and her other three siblings are married as well. "You can't compare and so your defences are up. What I have to say about things is less important. My opinions just don't count," Lori laments. God forbid you don't want to have children, god forbid you pursue a "slutty" lifestyle, prefer women, or simply wish to avoid men altogether! Of course, these choices are easier if family members aren't gossiping about your every move. This is why cities are a wonderful buffer zone — you can live in them anonymously. No one's going to complain because you're going to the movies in your pyjamas with three-day-old mascara running down your face, much less even give you a second glance. Because of this, the urban Italian girl fares much better than those in small towns; she can choose to be among her own kind. Here Friday night *Sex and the City* is as good as crack.

Assuming, of course, the single Italian girl doesn't live with her parents. If she does, the pressure to settle down may be too much to bear. Chances are, she'll make the grave mistake of marrying the first twit she sleeps with. He is her ticket out of her parents' house, a chance to buy her own furniture and to get out of the bedroom she's slept in since birth, an excuse to flaunt her sequinned thong on the doorknob rather than cramming it between mattress and boxspring.

As I pull into the driveway of my own parents' house, a driveway packed with cars, clusters of cousins visible through the window as they bend over the Genus III version of Trivial Pursuit at the dining room table, laughter almost audible from inside the car, my uncle literally roasting chestnuts on an open fire, and my grandmother watching *Three's Company* reruns, I know that I'll be embraced dozens of times over, my face smeared with lipstick. I'll be told how much I was missed, how much I'm loved. Who in their right mind would dare to complain about this? This unconditional outpouring, this privilege of support. "Why don't you move back to the Soo?" they'll ask. I'll smile to myself and cherish the sanctity of my Toronto apartment. Emphasis on *my*. This transit between two worlds suits me just fine. As I open the side door framed with blinking Christmas lights, I resolve to live with duplicity, to embrace it. Being single in an Italian family sometimes feels like wearing a bright-red nose to the opera, but the trick is to own the costume. Inhabit it long enough and soon you will find yourself in the company of other brave souls, and what good company it is.

Mamma

MARIA MONTINI

At 22, I, the daughter of Italian immigrants, left home. Before long, my father, my two brothers, and my dead mother had followed me.

I was born and raised in Ottawa; like so many in the 1950s, my parents immigrated to Canada to find the prosperity that had eluded them in post-World War II Italy. This country and their children came to be their promised land; in my two brothers and I, my parents glimpsed their future and their descendants.

My mother embraced her new life with gusto. Such heady dreams! Her boys would grow up to be *professori*, held up as great men within Ottawa's relatively small Italian community. I would get an education, but first and foremost I would marry *un dottore, un avvocato*. For this I would need what all Italian-Canadian girls pined for: a hope chest.

My mother regularly made the trip to Freiman's or Caplan's to be first in line for the White Sale. The competitors for this finery were no match for my mother, who had grown up with the wicked stepmother, Mamma Bologna, and who, with her brother and four sisters, had to fight for every egg and scrap of meat that came their way. With her broken English and gift for shoving her way to the front of the crowd, she would triumphantly return home with her treasure trove of bed sheets and tablecloths, declaring with a wink that these were for *quandu te faci monaca*, for when I became a nun.

My mother and my three aunts hovered over my hope chest, debating the best choices. Christmas and birthdays saw many gifts of pillowcases and tea towels. I thought all girls received linen on gift-giving holidays. My corruption began at school when I discovered that the Anglo-Canadian girls got not linens but toys for Christmas!

To my mother's great dismay, I declared I would be neither nun, nor wife. I wanted toys and, as I got older, books. My mother probably had her first heart attack the day she realized that I would never be properly domesticated.

However, it did not stop her from trying. In an effort to educate me on the finer points of sewing, she would recount the fables of *il Diaviolo e San Nicola* — The Devil and St. Nicholas. The devil, my mother told me, often appeared before San Nicola and challenged him to sewing duels. In spite of the temptation fo follow the devil's slothful ways, through persistence and patience, San Nicola always emerged the stitching champion. Her stories did not necessarily convince me of the need to strive for proficiency, but they did pass on the family tradition of story telling and, unintentionally perhaps, further kindled my love of books.

She watched me grow with alternating puzzlement and awe. There was no understanding my preference for books over cooking and keeping house. While taking a university biology course, I showed her pictures of fetal development and she wistfully noted, "I've had three children and you know more than I do." She fought my every step toward independence during those years, fearing she would lose me to boys, *l'Inglesi*, and a whole host of unknown demons.

When my Anglo-Canadian friends visited, she would sit nearby and assure us she just had some crocheting to finish, we weren't to worry about her. My friends, surprisingly, did not seem to mind. An abundance of Italian food was usually part of the deal. I longed for their white sandwiches and they feasted on my mother's lasagna.

When Trudeau became a fixture of Ottawa politics and multiculturalism took a firm hold, my Anglo-Canadian friend brought her Japanese boyfriend to my Italian household for dinner. With impeccable politeness, he nodded and took more food every time my mother commanded, "*Mangia.*" When he left, my mother remarked that he certainly had a healthy appetite. I later learned that the poor fellow had thrown up all night. My mother was hard to refuse.

I tried to ignore her efforts to keep my brothers and me close by. She regularly herded us to the Experimental Farm with its scores of flowers to have pictures taken of the three of us clutching the blooms. She insisted we attend every wedding, which gave her the opportunity to take more pictures of us holding flowers.

Then my parents bought the house next door, for us.

It was time to leave town. I had been accepted to both the University of Toronto and Western for grad school. London was further. My mother reluctantly accepted my need to travel to seek new horizons. After all, had she and her husband not done the same thing? She helped me prepare for my departure, but watched sadly as I boarded the train.

My first year away was marked by panicked phone calls when she could not reach me and uncharacteristically subdued conversation when she could. When she visited, she brought a suitcase so stuffed with salami and cheese it could not be carried by one person.

Gradually, my mother adjusted to my absence and her spunk returned, as did the boisterous extended family gatherings she loved. My parents celebrated their 25th wedding anniversary during my second year of grad school, in the spring of 1979, and my mother contentedly announced she would keep my father and not throw him out into the deep Ottawa snow after all. From a small seaside village in Apulia to *la vita bella* in America, we had all come a long way.

But that summer was to change everything. My mother died suddenly of a massive heart attack.

Months later, a *paesana* visited my father and quipped that his children had become *sparpaiati*, scattered like seeds in the wind to different parts of North America — my brothers to North Carolina and Calgary and me to Toronto, each of us finding escape for our own reasons.

I eventually married and had children and felt my mother's presence. When my youngest child was five and just learning to ride a bike, he fell from the sidewalk into the path of an oncoming truck. To my horror I could not reach him. Without warning, a woman reached down and placed him back on the sidewalk. As I rushed to my son, I turned to thank her, but she was gone. There were no side roads and no one in the distance. I like to think it was my mother.

Over the years, one by one, my family members found their way to Toronto. My brothers relocated to the city and by strange coincidence we found ourselves working for the same employer in the same region. Now the only member of my family left in Ottawa, my father decided he would make the move as well and came to live with me and my family. Four years later my brothers married and began families of their own. After some deliberation, my father decided my mother should join us too, and so he had her transferred to a cemetery nearby.

Now, amid the chaos of our own growing family

celebrations I have begun to understand my mother's hopes for her family in this country. I marvel at how my mother's spirit infuses her grandchildren, and how, mysteriously, though my brothers and I sought our own destinies, we have found ourselves in the same place.

An Affair to Remember

MARIA FRANCESCA LO DICO

I'm on the phone with my mamma during our daily call.
It's the middle of February and Montreal is experiencing
one of the worst deepfreezes in history. Temperatures
have dipped to -55°C with the wind chill factor and I tell
her I cannot fathom taking a shower because of the draft
in my bathroom.

"But Fra, you have to *wash*," she says. "Promise me you'll *wash*. This is why I have a bidet. Now you see how practical it is to have the bidet!"

My parents proudly installed the marble bidet when they built our house, a two-storey wonder of imported tile and marble finishings, a veritable Mediterranean villa nestled in quasi-arctic Montreal. On this chilly winter day, Mamma's bidet sounds downright brilliant because I would indeed like to wash without losing anything important to frostbite. Why hadn't Canadians thought of this?

When I was 16, that very same bidet represented everything that was "not normal" about my family. I had grown up believing that there was "Us" — *gli italiani* — and "Them"— *gli inglesi* (a.k.a. the rest of the world). As I began to question this divide, and before it ever crossed my mind that I could belong to both these worlds as a so-called "hyphenated Canadian," I tried to flip sides. Oh, the treachery!

I asked for an electric percolator because nobody on television drank espresso made with stove-top Mokas.

"Tastes like dirty water," my parents objected.

I asked for a subscription to the Montreal *Gazette* because TV families always got the paper delivered in the morning. I fantasized about having a newspaper route, but nobody in our neighbourhood read the newspapers put out by *gli inglesi*.

I laugh about this now, as a 36-year-old writer, and self-styled Sicilian goddess to boot. But when I moved out of the house to live on my own, my mamma "cried every day, every single day for a whole year she cried." This is how it is *still* described. I broke my mamma's heart and with every major decision I made, from choosing a career in the arts (and rejecting the family business, a successful flower shop), to remaining single, to refusing to move back home after my father died, I broke it again. I feared I would break it into so many pieces that eventually there would be nothing left but its hollowed out centre.

To further complicate matters, my mamma and I had never come to terms with what I now call "the original sin," a sin tailor-made for Sicilian-Catholic mamma-daughter guilt. This is how my mamma tells the story.

"We had just opened the shop — oh what unspeakable sacrifices to get the money — and I found myself pregnant. I was having trouble, so the doctor said to stay home, to stay in bed. But I couldn't afford to not work.

"Then you were born — such torturous labour — and I was sick, so sick, but I had to be at the shop every day from nine to three so your father could go to work at his day job. When he came to the shop, I went to work at the factory from three to midnight.

"So we sent you back to Sicily, to your father's parents. You learned to walk in Sicily, to say your first words in Sicily. When you came back, when I finally had you in my arms, you wanted *her*, Nonna. You wouldn't stop wailing for your grandmother. I can still hear your cries, feel you pushing me away. That moment of rejection was the most painful of my life. You cried for months. You wouldn't come near me *for months*."

Over the years, this story, often recited in the heat of a battle with my parents to elicit instant shame and guilt, has grown to mythical proportions. My mamma is the diva of her own opera and once, in the middle of an intense argument, she pulled out my baby book — which she had been forced to fill in relying on long-distance phone calls, letters, and photos from my nonna — and she began to read out passages in which she is tormented by my absence.

It was only when I was much older that I was able to deconstruct this story. I may have rejected my mamma, but I was a child traumatized by separation/abandonment twice over; and in her telling and retelling of the story, she was a mamma also traumatized by separation and guilt-ridden at having sent her baby away.

(My mamma had also carried a baby full-term who was stillborn and my younger brother was "blue when he was born," and almost didn't survive.) We remained locked in that moment well into my adulthood and managed to break free only when I went into therapy. (And here I can already hear readers gasping, "Good Italian girls do *not* go into therapy to rage at their mammas and reveal family secrets. Talk to your priest, *per la madonna!*")

Surprisingly, my mamma was open to the idea of therapy and even agreed to come to a session. We were settling down in Dr. Minde's office in posh anglo Westmount when it dawned on me that we had one serious roadblock. My mamma speaks Italian and a wee bit of French; Dr. Minde speaks only English. And so I found myself in a situation in which my mamma is very earnestly telling the therapist what she thinks is wrong with me — and I have to translate.

Oh, but it got worse. Afterwards, we had planned to shop for a winter coat, her Christmas present to me. I desperately needed a new one and she had offered to get me a full-length Kanuk, made-in-Quebec, top-of-the-line, absolutely fabulous parka insulated with handmade fibres, trimmed with polar fleece, able to withstand -30°C weather — a parka for superheroes. But after a joint therapy session, no mamma and daughter should ever go shopping together. The Marquis himself could not dream of anything more masochistic. All I could talk about to Dr. Minde from that moment forward was how much I hated that damn parka.

So how did the tragic melodrama of original sin become a romantic comedy about a daughter in love, truly in love, with her mamma? I took my mamma to an Aquafit class at the YMCA. She brought a fluffy white shower cap, which she insisted was the same as a swimming cap. "Those tight rubber things, they give me a headache, Fra." She wouldn't take off her glasses in the pool. "Fra, what if I get confused, forget where I am? What if I get lost? No, no, *lasciami stare.*" She did the class in shower cap and glasses, her head bobbing high above water the whole time. Afterwards, in the communal showers, she refused to take off her bathing suit in front of the other women so she washed as discreetly as possible with one hand buried in her cleavage! Far be it for me to dispute Sicilian modesty.

As we were dressing, I watched my mamma out of the corner of my eye, a voyeur of sorts. I was riveted by her 60-year-old body, riveted by the stories inscribed on her flesh, on the visible scars, in the varicose veins so sharply contrasted against the milkiness of her skin. I was mesmerized because I'd never taken a close look before, afraid perhaps that I'd see the wounds I'd inflicted on her.

My mamma broke the spell when she began to complain about the humidity in the changing room. "Fra, *staiu scattanù*," she said. Loosely translated, *scattanù* means to explode, self-combust, and die. "*Staiu veramente scattanù!* It's so hot, Fra. If we don't get out of here, I'm gonna self-combust, I'm gonna explode. I'm telling you I'm gonna die right here, right here. Fra, oh my God, I just died!"

My mamma dies 2.5 times a day, just as quickly and miraculously to rise from the ashes. She's kind of like Jesus Christ that way, my mamma the martyr.

In the throes of her final words, she had grabbed my arm with one hand while beating her chest with the other.

I said, "*Bo*, when's the funeral, 'cause I'm gonna wanna get one of those big funerary pieces spelling out M-A-M-M-A and those things take time."

That's when I realized my mamma and I were having a mad love affair. Our strongest bond, in the end, turned out to be a wicked sense of humour and the gift of gab. These are powerful tools for redressing the past, for reinventing it.

My family had believed that my interests in writing and intellectual pursuits came from my father. My mamma never read anything I had written because it was in English, while my father read both English and French. But I was my mamma's daughter too, and had inherited the gift of comedy from her, a masterful storyteller who recently dissed her nemesis by saying, "That nun may eat Christ, but she shits the Devil!"

~

In 2003, just before Christmas, Mamma called me. "I just wanted you to know that I've decided to write about my life. I know what you're thinking, that I'm an illiterate peasant, and it's true, I am. But I sit here and I think to myself: have I really lived through all these things? Every morning I remember and I jot down my memories; I have a system. Right now, I'm only doing up to 10 years old, my birth to 10. Is that how you do it, Fra? Is that how you write?"

Imagine how revolutionary this was in a culture that proclaims, "We Italians, we work with our hands." Here was a Sicilian mamma saying to her rebel daughter, "You are an example to me, *carisimma figlia*." I cried, I cried, I cried for a week, I cried.

This is my mamma's life. She gets her hair done once a week, on Friday mornings, at Salon Moda. It's a right of passage, this luxury. All the other ladies get the same do, a gravity-defying, perfectly shaped helmet. The buzz from the hairspray keeps them high for days, Mamma's head bobbing erratically until it wears off. She also sleeps with a protective pair of stretched "underwears" over her head. A couple of times she's forgotten to take them off before leaving the house.

One of her favourite pastimes is going to the Montreal Casino with her friends. She talks about it in whispers because she doesn't want to be labelled a "lady of the casino." She's been very lucky and when I asked to borrow money to buy a new computer, she said, "I'll take you to the casino and win you the money."

The women from the salon and casino are obsessed with dreams as well as winning and regularly consult my mamma's copy of *I Sogni*, an Italian book on dream interpretation. They're particularly interested in how to translate the dreams into numbers for 6/49 Lotto Quebec.

But my mamma is at her most formidable at Fiorista San Remo, the flower shop she built with my father and brother. She may be an "illiterate peasant," but at San Remo she is simply *la signora la fiorista*. Everybody knows her and she knows everybody. Ask her for a reference about so-and-so, and she'll sum them up with: "Good people. They always pay their bills on time."

The flower shop is across the street from Notre Dame de la Consolata Church, so for almost four decades *la signora la fiorista* has been a part of countless baptisms, weddings, and funerals. The funerals, especially, are important because Italians love honouring their dead. It's not just tradition, it's a life's work.

What makes my mamma formidable is her unique business acumen. Let me set the scene: It's Easter, one of the busiest times of the year for a flower shop, and I am helping. So are my cousins, aunts, and uncles. Signora Ciccirillo (she's old school and has been living in the neighbourhood for decades) wants to buy a $3.99 hyacinth. She comes up to the cash and I punch it in: $4.29 with taxes.

"No!" says Mrs. Ciccirillo. "Me, I never pay taxes."

"But Mrs. Ciccirillo, everybody pays taxes."

"No! Me, I never pay taxes. Where's *la signora la fiorista*? *La signora la fiorista* never makes me pay taxes."

"Okay, Mrs. Ciccirillo, she's in the back. You're gonna have to wait."

"My bus is coming. I haven't got all day."

Meanwhile, Signor Valle has come up to the cash with a hibiscus in a basket. "I'm gonna buy this, but I'm not paying for the basket."

"But Mr. Valle, the basket alone is worth $6.50."

"No, tell *la signora la fiorista* that Niccolo Valle is here, and me, I never pay taxes."

Ten minutes later, Mrs. Ciccirillo has missed two buses: "*La signora la fiorista*, she's forgotten about me?"

"Mrs. Ciccirillo, it's the busiest time of the year for us. She'll be here in a second."

"But my bus . . ."

Niccolo pipes up, "You know, I'm taking this to the cemetery. Tell *la signora la fiorista* it's for the cemetery, for my wife, Ninetta. Did you tell her Niccolo Valle is here?"

So Mamma came up with a plan. I brought in an old computer screen, plopped it on the counter. Wasn't even plugged into anything. And whenever a Mrs. Ciccirillo or a Mr. Valle would say the dreaded, "Me, I never pay taxes," my mamma would point to the computer and say, "But we're computerized now. Everything is on the computer. I can't fiddle with anything. My son is manager now. You know, these kids, *la vita moderna*, our old ways don't work anymore, there's nothing I can do."

And as soon as the old-timers heard the words "*il computere*," it was like putting the fear of god into them. "Oh, *il computere*," they'd whisper and cough up the taxes.

My mamma, she's got a head for business, all right, all kinds of business. Recently, after one of our Aquafit classes, we decide to have *una brekfesta quebecese* (Quebecois breakfast). First, we dropped by a Greek fish and seafood store where my mother had an orgasm upon seeing a mountain of fish heads for sale. "Fra, is this possible? Madonna!" Needless to say, my mother loves a good fish head and "They're so hard to find, *per carita*." She goes on an impressive shopping spree, buying enough shrimp, salted cod, squid and skatewing to keep myself, my brother, and his wife happy as clams for weeks. The fish heads she kept all for herself.

We were settling into our booth at a local greasy spoon when our talk turned to babies. "It would be nice," said my mamma, "if your brother would start a family soon. I'd like to be a nonna. I'm ready. But it's none of our business. No, no, none of our business, Fra. I'm not one of those overbearing mammas. No, no, that's not me. It's up to Angelo and Geraldine. It's their business and theirs alone."

For years now, I had been pining for a baby of my own. It was no secret that I loved children, but I was in my mid-30s, single, and not sure I could handle parenthood alone.

"Fra, I've been *thinking*. You of all people should have a baby. *Ho propio questio desiderio.* Have a baby, Fra. I'll help you. Oh, how I would help you. However you want to have it, it's your choice. Adopt! You could adopt.

Imagine a little Chinese baby speaking our Sicilian dialect. How I would love it!"

Yes, I am a woman head over heels in love with her mamma. It's a thoroughly modern arrangement. We live apart. We have separate lives. But we are thinking of having a baby together. *Mamma mia!*

Thicker Than Water

ANNA NOBILE

The photographs fascinated me. Even at a young age, I loved taking down the shoebox full of black-and-white stills from its place high on the closet shelf.

"That's your Zio Silvano," my mother said.

"He looks so young."

"He was just a boy then. See, here, he's taking you on his *bicicletta* for some *gelato*."

Aunts, uncles, grandparents. Birthdays, anniversaries, weddings. It hardly seemed possible that a shoebox could hold so much life.

"Who's that?"

"*Non lo conosci?* You don't recognize him? That's your father on crutches when he broke his leg on the job. Everybody was good to us then, helping us out."

There were many baby pictures of me and my sister. Even at ten years of age I could not imagine being that small. There's one of my father holding me in my baptismal dress. I have a pinched look on my face, as if I've just tasted something sour.

"Look how beautiful you are," my mother said, oblivious to my funny face. "Your papà was so happy when you were born. He went to everybody's house handing out cigars," she chuckled. "It's good to know your history, to know your family."

Photo: Vancouver. I have been living here for two years. The day is sunny and warm and I'm sitting in the park with Anne and Cindy listening to the grrl bands. Behind us, two men are kissing. This anniversary of the 1969 Stonewall Riots never fails to bring out the queer community en masse, in all its diversity. Though we have gained a handful of civil rights in the last thirty years, the struggle is not over: books continue to be banned; we are still bashed, killed.

Today, though, we take a break, give ourselves time to celebrate. The band starts to play "We Are Family" and everybody gets up and sings.

Growing up in Toronto had its advantages. It was a big city with many distractions, many cultures; the Italian-Canadian community alone was a half-million strong. Belonging to such a large population was a double-edged sword; it was comforting knowing I wasn't alone, but suffocating knowing there were few places to hide. My parents would often remind me that we were *tutti paesani*. This accounted for the photographs of individuals who weren't, strictly speaking, related to us, and for the people who came to stay with us after they first emigrated. Our house became a way station for newcomers, a place for them to find their footing before moving on. We were all Italians, we were all family, no questions asked.

By the time I was a teenager, the influx of *paesani* had abated, and our social circle took in primarily extended family. Around this time, the photos switched to colour and the shoebox was set aside in favour of proper albums. My mother organized the photos by theme or event. I preferred going through the shoebox because you never knew what picture would come next. The albums contained many embarrassing pictures of me: on the swings, my face covered in ice cream; making my first snowman; at my first Communion; surrounded by Italian Easter eggs. After my sister came along, these scenes were repeated, though they now featured the two of us.

Photo: Pacific Rim Park. Kira leans against the tree she has just fallen out of. She's in shock and has broken her pelvis. We will know this only after the ordeal of getting her up the steep trail to the car. She insists I take her picture. We cannot leave until I take her picture. I try to hurry her along, one arm around me, the other using a branch as a crutch. The sun is setting and it is getting cold. Every few minutes she asks me what time it is. She will forget these details, as she will the long wait in emergency, the ride home, the safety of bed. Soon after, we become lovers.

I graduated from the University of Toronto in 1986, the first person in my family to do so. This was rather unexpected. Many photos were taken and sent back to *i nonni*, proof of the family's success in Canada. The pressure mounted to go on to bigger and better things: a car, a house, a husband.

I told my parents, and anyone else who would listen, that I would never marry. Of course, no one listened. Only I could hear the voice that said, "You are different." When I fell in love with a blonde, blue-eyed woman of

Irish-Hungarian descent who wanted to travel, being different posed a serious dilemma. Should I tell my family and risk the certainty of their rejection or lead a double life?

Throughout my early 20s, I lied about the nature of my relationship. We were "best friends," a schoolyard term that could never represent the whole truth. Lies were easier, but only slightly. I wasn't disowned, merely displaced. I couldn't talk about it, couldn't seek advice from my mother when my lover and I quarrelled.

I stopped attending family gatherings, partly because I stopped identifying myself as a family member and partly because I could never bring the person who most mattered to me. I skipped showers and weddings. Part of me was relieved. I was saving a lot of money, I told myself, not having to buy wedding presents or make donations to the *bustina*. Besides, did I really want to participate in ceremonies that only emphasized my isolation? I passed up opportunities to go on weekend camping trips, to attend birthday and anniversary parties. I was on the outside.

Part of me was silenced. I could never talk about what I truly thought and felt, could never participate fully in my family's life, nor they in mine. The ceremonies and celebrations that marked the passage of time went on without me. I slowly disappeared from my family's photographs.

It was only a matter of time before I disappeared altogether.

Photo: Vancouver. Kira and me on the balcony. She has been travelling and we haven't seen each other for three months. She sits on my lap. We look into each other's eyes and the camera clicks just as we are about to kiss. I have stocked the house with her favourite foods, prepared rice balls and peach pie. In the morning I will deliver Italian cookies and caffè latte. She is home.

In June 1990, I left Toronto and moved to Vancouver. My parents preferred to think of it as an emigration. This was a concept they could grasp, having done it themselves. I was going west to seek my fortune. This helped reconcile loss with reality, though I suspect my parents had long conversations in private. They wished me well, and then told everyone my company had transferred me to Vancouver. In fact, I had quit. I was furious. Did they have to lie about everything I did? Was I really so outrageous? Once they lied, I felt obliged to go along with it rather than embarrass them further. I just needed room to grow, space to breathe, yet this somehow translated into shameful behaviour.

"But, they won't understand," my mother pleaded, trying to make me see reason.

"You're leaving the family," my father said, anger in his voice.

Mamma, Papà, I cannot leave something that has abandoned me.

Released from the chains of my parents' expectations and the need to maintain appearances, I am able to fully be myself. But sharing my life with my family is still impossible. My private life is never discussed, but, to make matters worse, I'm not sure they notice. I have become a master of evasion, adept at leaving out details I'm certain will be met with disbelief.

Photo: Vancouver. Me in my new jeans, holding Baci, my cat. I send it to my parents to give them some idea of my life. I bought the new jeans with the money they sent me for my birthday. I look a little tired. I'm working hard on my master's thesis and not getting enough sleep. On the back of the photo I write: Thanks for the new jeans. Anna. Like them, I don't write "love."

My father died two years after I moved to Vancouver. By that time, we were strangers to each other. Even before I moved, we hadn't talked much, but then my mother's attempts to keep the family together forced us into each other's company at least once a week over a traditional

Sunday meal. After I left to forge a new life in Vancouver, I found I had nothing to say to him. Telephone conversations became strained.

Photo: Toronto. My niece, Lisa, has turned six. She is sitting at my mother's kitchen table with one of my mother's famous cakes in front of her. Beside her are her sister, her mother, and her father. Except for Lisa, who is intent on blowing out her candles, the others look tentatively into the camera. My brother-in-law looks especially uncomfortable. I wonder about all the things this photo doesn't tell me. I wonder who these people are.

My father's death has been hard on my mother. My sister is busy raising her girls, and I'm on the other side of the country, as she never fails to remind me. She usually calls to relay news about an uncle having heart surgery, a cousin having a second baby, a *paesana* down the street who uses a cane now.

"Uh-huh," I reply to everything.

"You're not listening," she says sharply, during one such conversation.

I hesitate. "No," I admit finally.

"They're your family," she counters. "You should know what's going on in their lives."

"I'm family too," I said, suddenly irritated. "Don't you want to know what's going on in my life?"

"Sure I do."

"Then why don't you ask?"

"So? Tell me. What are you doing?"

So I tell her. Or at least I try to. I would like to say more but all I can manage is my usual litany — work, school, friends. We'd stopped talking, really talking, years ago, and now we can't seem to find our way back to that easier time.

"Hey, Ma? Whatever happened to that shoebox?"

"What shoebox?"

"You know. The one with all the pictures in it."

"Oh, *qui lo sa?* Probably in the basement somewhere. Why?"

"Just wondering."

Photo: Vancouver. Me in my master's cap and gown, laughing, surrounded by all my friends — my family of choice. They are wearing caps too, lest I get too high and mighty. After much deliberation, I had decided not to invite my mother to the ceremony. Instead, I sent her a photo looking properly sombre in my scholar's robes.

I have travelled three thousand miles in order to live a life that is not a lie, which is filled with caring, like-minded people. From this distance, my mother can be proud of whatever "successes" I share with her, and the things she doesn't want anyone else to know are easily hidden, denied. Any closer and her shame would be too much for me to bear. She would have to lie again. I could say that leaving behind a family that forced me to hide and deny myself for one that loves and embraces me has been worth the sacrifice, but the dulling of love with shame and guilt, absence and loss, has cost us both. I miss my mother and I believe she misses me as well.

Photo: A group shot of me and all my friends, and my mother, at the Gay Pride Parade. My mother and I will have our arms around each other. She will visit one day, perhaps soon, and will meet all my friends. She will hesitate a bit, but they will soon have her casting all her prejudices aside. She didn't know lesbians could be so much fun. My friends will take an instant liking to her. She is, after all, a wonderful cook and a captivating story-teller. She will take this photo home with her and find a place for it in the family album.

My parents paid the price of passage to get here, then paid the price of loneliness and isolation to stay. Eventually, enough family and *paesani* came over that they built a *famiglia* — a community of blood relations that could be relied upon in bad times, as well as good. My experience of immigration has been much the same. I have forged lasting friendships in my adopted city, built close ties with people who love and respect me for who I am. Yet none of these people are, strictly speaking, family. Blood may be thicker than water, but it's water that will quench a thirst.

Anabelle's Dumb Wedding

NETTA RONDINELLI

Anabelle was only 18 when she declared she was marrying the only guy she'd ever dated. No doubt she thought she was buying her freedom because until the announcement she hadn't been allowed to go out, not even *with* her boyfriend.

I, on the other hand, was free to play and come and

go as I pleased because I wasn't a woman yet. All my friends were wearing bras and had gotten their periods, some had even received bouquets of roses for their entry into womanhood. All this repulsed me. I swore that I wouldn't tell Mamma when it happened to me because that would mean I'd get *biancheria*, or *linens* to fill my hope chest instead of real presents on my birthday. Anabelle's chest was already full.

Mamma and Papa told Anabelle she was being too hasty. They were disappointed that she had chosen this instead of pursuing her dream to become a lawyer, but at least she agreed to complete her degree. Mamma and Papa didn't get married until they were in their mid-20s — that was considered old by Italian standards.

My parents might not have been happy with Anabelle's news, but I was. This was finally my chance to be in a bridal party. I wasn't keen on wearing heels or anything pretty, but I would finally have an opportunity to show everyone who I was. Mamma's *paesani* had forgotten that I existed — I always had to remind them that I was the *seconda* and a *girl*.

I was rifling through Anabelle's purse looking for gum when I stumbled upon a black wedding organizer with tabs containing a goldmine of information. Under the pink tab for Bridesmaids are four similar sounding names — cousin Angela, cousin Angie, his cousin Angela, and Angelica — but no mention of mine. What was Anabelle thinking? My cousin Angelica over me? She was only nine months older than I was, but she was more mature, she had breasts and a waist. I tore through every tab, including Ushers, looking for mine but found only Joe, Joey, Joseph, cousin Gio, and Giuseppe. I was pissed. I wanted revenge. I vowed to set my fat-ass sister straight.

I pulled out her box of giant Kotex pads and peeled back the adhesives. I stuck 10 lilac-scented, super absorbent ones on the bottom of her tote bag. This didn't make me feel any better, but I was so *self*-absorbed that I didn't hear Anabelle walk in only to find me with my sticky fingers in her purse.

"What the fuck did I tell you about going through my things, you little twit?" she said as she pinched me.

"I don't care what you told me! I'll be glad when you're gone, you ass!" I shouted and ran off to tell my parents.

My parents were too *preoccupati* figuring out who would be invited to the engagement party and determining a proper location to pay attention to me. Anabelle had gone out again, so I snuck into her room. I rummaged through her make-up bag and searched for her cherry-scented lipgloss. I found four green speckled pills in a tin case. What could they be? Pills to make her skinny? Like that was ever going to happen.

I pulled my father aside and showed him the pills, out of concern, and said that I had found them while I was cleaning. I could see that he didn't recognize them, and my father knew everything. I told him that I found them on her dresser and I thought they might be vitamins. Papa didn't buy it. He took the pills and put them in his jacket pocket. "Hmmm," he said. No more, no less. Papa wasn't a man of few words. Anabelle was in trouble.

He told Mamma he was going to the pharmacy. When he got back I took advantage of his mood and told him that I wasn't even a bridesmaid.

He didn't seem to care and blurted instead, "If I find out that your sister's having sex before she gets married, I'm not going to pay for that goddamn dress!"

Just the thought of Anabelle having sex grossed me out. Papa must not have brought it up with Anabelle because she continued her wedding plans, including designing our "honorary dresses." Anabelle designed matching teal-and-white, ruffled, taffeta dresses with scalloped edges for Louise and me.

I had tried confronting Annabelle about my role in the wedding, but she had the gall to turn the tables on me. "You don't even wear dresses, why do you care?" she hissed.

Anabelle was right, I didn't wear dresses and I didn't particularly care for the dusty rose silk ones the bridesmaids had to wear, but it was my biological right to at least be *asked*.

The day before the wedding, Anabelle had left very specific instructions for me. I was in charge of handing out headpieces to the bridesmaids. How hard could it be? Papa laughed and said a monkey could do the job. But, as I said, the bridesmaids' names were all very similar and as, one by one, the "Angs" dropped by to pick up their pink floral headpieces, I began to get confused. Even though Angie insisted she had one at home, I made her take it. When Angelica arrived and there were none to be found I was as dumbfounded as she was. Math was not my strong suit.

Anabelle was furious, she couldn't figure out where she had gone wrong. She spent the rest of that afternoon racing from store to store, frantically searching for a duplicate headpiece. When she finally came home and realized that I given her stupid fiancée's cousin two head pieces — she freaked. She locked herself in her bedroom and refused to speak to anyone. Only my grandmother was granted permission to enter. Anabelle was named after my grandmother. I could hear my sister sobbing and going on about what a disaster the wedding day was going to be.

I was starting to feel a little remorseful. I hadn't realized how badly I'd screwed things up. I pressed my ear to her bedroom door.

"Don't worry Anabelle," I heard Nonna say, "these people are stupid. Everything will be perfect tomorrow. You'll see." Anabelle stormed out of her bedroom with her wedding dress crumpled in a big white ball and threw it on the front lawn.

"How the fuck am I supposed to wear this dress? It's wrinkled for fuck's sakes." Mamma had picked up Anabelle's dress that morning and hung it in her tiny closet. Anabelle's tears continued to stream and she started panting.

Nonna carefully picked up the dress. The Spanish styled lace was smushed but she hung it from the chandelier.

On the day of the wedding Louise and I looked like the loser sisters, Brigitta and Louisa from *The Sound of Music*. My cousins laughed at me and told me I looked like a lampshade. There was no honour in the dress, except for the fact that it masked the stinking maxi pad I had to wear. I woke up that morning with soiled underwear. I had to keep this to myself because I didn't want to steal Anabelle's thunder or alert my mother. I found the Kotex and it was easy enough to figure things out from there.

But what really stunk about the day was that Louise and I didn't even get to wear corsages. A meddling cousin decided to give our rose-coloured carnations to distant cousins from Niagara Falls instead. No one noticed.

Messing with the Malocchio

IVANA BARBIERI

It hits me sometime between the antipasto and the tomato-and-cream pasta. A creeping sensation crawls up my spine and then my temples begin to throb. I manage to tolerate it until my fellow diners polish off the pork medallions, but once the sherbet arrives, I can barely lift my head. I snake my way through the ceramic swans in the banquet hall and head directly for the ladies' room. I splash cold water on my face and reach for the codeine, hoping it will do the trick. I cross my fingers, down two, and decide to wait twenty minutes. With any luck, I won't have to go to Plan B (*malocchio*).

Back at the table, everyone is well into the fifth (or is it the sixth?) course — the hot fish and salad. Knowing looks pass among them. Still feeling flushed, I pierce a steamed mussel. By mid-August, you'd think they'd have proper air conditioning in a fancy place like this. I pass on the seafood and fan myself with my place card. My head is still pulsing. The fruit course is on its way.

My mother is the first to notice. She leans over to her brother seated on her right and asks him to do the "eye."

"*S'fascina.*" Zio sets his prickle pear aside and makes a subtle sign of the cross on his forehead. Uh oh. Just as I suspected — Plan B.

The evil eye is a small-c curse. It is generally unintentional and caused by someone praising, complimenting, or looking enviously at her victim. The hex can work on livestock and crops, but babies and old people are particularly susceptible. I scan the room for potential offenders. The rest of the table has caught on. We all watch my uncle intently, waiting for the gesture guaranteed to follow. If he yawns, I'm in trouble.

He tries to stifle it. Affirmative.

"Well, so much for the codeine," I grumble, not looking forward to the nausea that would follow premature medication.

"You should know by now that you can't cure a *malocchio* headache with Tylenol," Zia retorts between bites of tiramisu. I resist the urge to correct her as Zio murmurs through the obligatory incantations.

"I forgot the salt," my mother adds as she prepares a makeshift amulet with the saltshaker and a cloth napkin. Normally, on such occasions, I carry a piece of rock salt wrapped in tin foil in my evening bag — an evil-eye buffer. It works especially well at job interviews, in the pocket of my business suits for good luck, and to intercept bad vibes. I place the stand-in amulet in my purse.

"I remembered the *mutandine*," I declare in my defence. Although skeptical, I go along with this tradition passed on from my Sicilian grandmother. Red underwear. They are to be worn on New Year's Eve and on other social occasions for added protection. Nonna was a firm believer that someone, a *jettadore*, could deliberately cast the *malocchio* on anyone or anything whom they deemed attractive, intelligent, or successful. She always said the best *jettadores* were blue-eyed and should never be trusted. Blue eyes were so rare in the south that they were seen as a paranormal invasion connected to Celtic intruders in the north. *Jettadores* wreak vengeance on behalf of jealous or envious third parties, 15th-century justice for vendettas against petty village squabbles.

"*Masculo o femina?*" my mother inquires as Zio finishes the prayer ritual.

"*Masculo,*" he replies. A male inflictor.

My sister guesses the bartender at cocktail hour and my mother guesses the usher in the receiving line who complimented me on my sandals. My bet is that friend of my cousin, up from the States, who showered me with compliments and intense gazes just long enough to get reacquainted. I have vague memories of him at football games before the brain drain took him south of the border. I had managed to catch him up — my mom and sister were fine, work was great, no *fidanzato* or boy-friend, but all things considered everything was superb.

"Bogus or not, all I know is that when I get one of those migraines, a phone call to Zio does the trick," my sister vows over her latté *macchiato*. "Weddings are perfect for the *facina*. Good news can be bad news if you've landed a great new job, lost weight, or gotten a new haircut," she adds, speaking from experience.

After dessert, the guests are free to roam the ballroom and reacquaint themselves with the *paesani* they rarely see, except at weddings and funerals. Three so far. It's been a slow year.

"Speaking of haircuts," my cousin Sonia chuckles "and of *malocchio*, did my mother ever tell you what happened during my first trip to Sicily? I must have been two or three. My parents took a trip to the village. I was all rosy cheeks and ringlets and people were always stopping to coo at me in supermarkets and at bus stops. One evening just as my father stooped to lift me over the *terrazza* into my mother's waiting arms, we heard moans coming from the adjacent corral. Lidia, my grandfather's mule, had not eaten in two days, a sure symptom of *l'occhio*.

"'Where are you going?' Nonna inquired, aligning two chairs on her terrace with a perfect view over the town square. She prided herself on knowing the next day's gossip ahead of Ciccirinella, the town know-it-all.

"'*A Milazzo*,' Dad cut in before my mother could reply. We had just planned a leisurely walk in the *piazza*, but my mother went along with Dad's white lie. Nonna was notorious for tagging along and would not be up for the one-hour trek to the adjacent town and back.

"'*Aspetta*. I'm coming too.' She disappeared into her house for her shawl even though it was close to forty degrees outside.

"'*Maladetta*,' my father whispered under his breath.

"Nonna returned not with her shawl, but with a pair of pinking shears. She scampered down the balcony stairs and hacked off a sizeable chunk of my golden locks, bows and all!

"'*Sei pazza?* What are you doing?' my father hollered, as Nonna dashed back into the house and secured the lock of my hair in her ancient hope chest for safekeeping. My mother burst into tears and reneged on the evening stroll.

"Ever since my twin brother died, Nonna had been convinced that I was the sorcerer's apprentice. Twins always have the 'gift,' so Nonna honestly believed that my hair could restore the mule's good health. Sure enough, Lidia bounced back and lived another five years. Nobody knows what became of the wisp of hair, but I'll bet Nonna stashed it somewhere. I don't think my father talked to her for the remainder of the trip. The next day, we packed our bags and headed for Calabria.

"But I'm protected now," Sonia laughs as she produces a tiny gold bull's horn from a chain around her neck. "I read somewhere that it's a bull's horn because an ancient pagan goddess had a bull as her consort."

"Last summer in Italy I found the plastic variety all over the place," my sister pipes in. "They're sold in open-air markets to hang on the front doors. One *bancarella* specialized in the real thing: hot red peppers strung into garlands and hung to dry in the sun. Like garlic, the pungency of the spice is meant to keep the parasites at bay."

"*Facitivi corni!*" my mother warns as Comare Concetta makes her way to our table. Our hands dive under the tablecloth as we assume the defensive position. Middle fingers and thumbs curled in, forefinger and baby finger extended. You mess with the bull, you get the horns.

I really don't know why we call her Comare. She's nobody's godmother, not even by confirmation. Not that she means any real harm, but her digs at my parents' divorce and our subsequent "success" always inspire an inner rolling of the eyes.

"*L'invidia e il piu brutto dei peccati.*" She preaches that envy is the worst of all sins as we listen politely. "I love everyone, but someone has put a curse on me." She promises she is never jealous. She vows that she is never envious. She swears that she has never sinned against others. But how is it that this year her garden has not produced a single tomato, or one lousy zucchini? Might it be due to the death of her mother, the sadness lodged deep within her heart? We exchange pleasantries. We compliment one another on our outfits and hear how her granddaughter has just paid down a sizeable chunk of her mortgage. She makes a date with Zio for an expulsion.

My sister and I surround our uncle and inquire about the de-cursing process. "We'll just call you the zucchini exorcist. What is it you actually do, Zio?" I ask.

"I can't tell you," he replies.

"Why not?"

"Not until midnight mass, Christmas Eve. When the priest raises the large host before last blessing, sit with me," he dismisses us as he reaches for a cigarette and lights up. Zio frowns upon handing down these rites of passage. I click my tongue impatiently.

Zia Angela, who is visiting from Calabria for the first family wedding *"intra Merica,"* sadly shakes her head. I fib and tell her that my headache's fading and the air conditioning seems to be working again, but she is not convinced.

"It's because we are so happy. Something was bound to come along and jinx us, jinx this happiness. God never lets us be happy for too long," she wails. I pull my *pashmina* over my shoulders as she hauls me to the ladies' room.

Zia runs the hot water and plugs the sink. She produces a small flask of olive oil from her purse and pours three drops into the sink while making the sign of the cross. *"In nome del cielo, delle stelle e della luna, mi levo questo malocchio per tua maggior fortuna."* she whispers. She gestures three crosses with her right hand over my forehead.

I try to protest.

"Zita!" The oil widens over the surface of the water, confirming that I have been stricken. Zia pulls a *fazzoletto* from her bra and mops her sweaty brow. It is worse than she thought. The moon and the stars are not responding. She is going to have to call on Jesus, Joseph, Mary, and the saints. Talk about divine intervention.

"Gesǔ, Giuseppe, y Maria si cé il malocchio mandatelo via; in nome di tutti i Santi il malocchio no va avanti; in nome di San Marco y San Pietro il malocchio torna in dietro; e Santíssima Trinitá abbiate voi pietá; Santíssima Concezione, questo malocchio vada in perdizione!" Jesus, Joseph, and Mary can send the evil eye packing. Saint Mark and Saint Paul will whack it with *uno bello schiaffo* and the Holy Trinity will show mercy.

Zia repeats the prayers three times until the dribbles start to congeal in one place. She is still not won over. I want her to stop, but I am feeling too weak as she half drags me to the kitchen signalling to her brother. Zio follows in hot pursuit.

The brother-sister tag team are all set up. Zio has the olive oil and the water is boiling on the stove. Zia Angela produces a sewing kit. Who knew she was a witch?

"Malochje n'genzate, tre sande m'aiutate, che poss'i nt'a l'occhje, a cchi e fatte nu malocchje." If she's speaking dialect you know she's pissed.

Thrice.

Nothing.

Zio takes over. He inserts the tip of one needle into the eye of the other. Zia resumes.

"Occhio e malocchio e cornicelli agli occhi, crepa la invidia e schiattono gli occhi. Lunedi Santo, Martedi Santo, Mercoledi Santo, Giovedi Santo, Venerdi Santo, Sabato Santo, e Domenica di Pasqua, il malocchio casca!" I'm vaguely reminded of Good Friday mass as Zio drops the needles into a casserole along with three pinches of salt. He jabs the scissors, once, twice, three times, and hacks away at the air above the stainless steel Lagostina.

"Basta." He stops. The spell is broken. "Thank goodness."

I regain my composure and make it back in time to join the conga line's fifth whirl around the ballroom dance floor. Zia gathers up her goodies and Zio lines up at the dessert table.

"Hey." My cousin's ex-pat friend has miraculously appeared at my side. I managed to dodge his earlier attempts at a tarantella but the band's playing a song by

Umberto Tozzi "Shall we?" He winks as he leads me to the dance floor. He has blue eyes.

I'm smitten, but not taking any chances. Just to be on the safe side, my left hand snakes behind my back as I give the *mano corni* one last try.

Four Weddings and a Funeral

NANCY KINDY

WEDDING #1:
FIDEL AND REGINA, AUGUST 1941,
ST. LEO'S CHURCH, MIMICO, ONTARIO

They lived next door to each other as teenagers. My father had 12 siblings; my mother had 6. After a few years in Australia with his brother Rocco, Fidel, a handsome man with thick, dark wavy hair and much sought after by the local girls, returned to Canada and to courting. Rumour had it that he planned to marry one of these candidates, but instead he asked out Regina, and then asked her widowed mother, Erminia, for her daughter's hand in marriage.

Erminia said, "You have my blessing. You are a good man, a hard worker, and my husband said three years ago that if you ever wanted to marry Regina he would give his blessing."

The wedding reception was a small affair with family and close friends, held at Erminia's modest home. The table was overflowing with homemade pasta dishes. The younger brothers and sisters, dressed in their Sunday best, comforted Erminia, who wished her husband could be there to share in the joy. She spent all her time in the kitchen cooking, cleaning, and serving the neighbours who stopped by to offer their congratulations and stay for food and drink.

A few years after their marriage, Fidel and Regina moved to the small town of Humber Summit, north of Mimico. They purchased a few acres of land and bought a house from a family in the village, which they moved onto the property until Fidel could build a new home.

They had three children; I was the only girl and we were the only Italian-Canadians in the community.

When we visited my father's parent's home, my grandfather sat me down beside him and in broken English told me stories of his boyhood days in Italy, how he would take his dog and go into the mountains to gather the sheep. Tired and hungry, he would pick berries and he and the dog would survive off the land. I protested that dogs didn't eat berries, but his eyes just twinkled with laughter and he continued more animated than before. When my grandfather finished his story he said, "Whata me say?" and I would repeat the story exactly as he told it, word for word. If I embellished or forgot a detail he would stop me and I would have to start again. My grandfather's name was Antonio Giorgio. Upon arriving in Canada in the 1920s he was told his name would henceforth be Tony George. Consequently, our surname bore no signs of our Italian heritage. My parents sounded English and they spoke English; they could speak and understand Italian as well, but they didn't see the need for their children to learn it.

Meanwhile, Erminia greeted us with open arms and put on a pot of chicken soup if we arrived at lunchtime. We had to eat, even if we weren't hungry. *"Mangia,*

mangia!" she would say over the sounds of her friends playing bingo. They slapped the table and fought over pennies, then chatted over coffee and desserts and parted good friends.

But back in Humber Summit no one spoke Italian, so I became totally Canadian again. In school I endured my music teacher, who pronounced the title of the song "Santa Lucia" with a "c." I boldly raised my hand and said, "It's pronounced Lucia with a 'ch.'" He laughed and asked if I was Italian. When he questioned the name George my shy defence had none of the confidence I'd had moments before. I didn't tell him the Giorgio-George story; he had embarrassed me enough in front of my classmates. I didn't admit to being Italian again. It was the end of WWII and Italy was on the wrong side in the war. My mother and other Italian women had been fired from a canning factory in fear that the Italian workers would poison the soup. My mother had been born in Canada, but that didn't matter to the managers. Her Italian heritage had lost her a job and I felt a similar prejudice that day in the classroom.

I didn't want to be an Italian and I didn't want to be a girl. I was convinced that a boy's life was much more interesting. After all, boys could grow up to be men who went to work, played cards, fished, and worked on cars.

My mother looked after the house and children, cooked and cleaned and served her husband. She didn't even drive a car. Later I discovered her secret yearning to be a nurse. She had had to go to work at a young age to support her widowed mother and her six siblings. When she was of age it was expected that she should marry and have her own children. As the provider, my father argued that a woman's place was in the home.

Because I was the only girl, and because I wanted to be more like my father than my mother, I became a daddy's girl, riding in his big red dump truck or the yellow bulldozer in the gravel pit. This was the ultimate treat — better than candy. My mother tried to teach me things in the kitchen, but when I showed no interest she didn't insist. "She'll learn in time," she would say.

WEDDING #2:

BRIAN AND NANCY, SEPTEMBER 1970,

ST. JUDE'S ROMAN CATHOLIC CHURCH,

WESTON, ONTARIO

But in 1969 daddy's girl met a man. He was tall, good looking, confident to the point of being cocky, but he was not Italian, nor was he Catholic. "What nationality is

Brian?" my father asked. When I told him that Brian wasn't sure himself, he was shocked. "A man should know his roots."

Brian and I got engaged in April the following year and married in September. Brian agreed to marry Catholic, but did not understand why the church classed us as a "mixed marriage." We went to marriage classes to reconcile the fact that he was a non-Catholic. Brian attended the classes reluctantly.

When I met Brian's parents they were very cordial and welcomed me into their family. I didn't look Italian and Nancy George didn't sound Italian. Nonetheless, his mother said, "If Brian's Grandmother Kindy were alive today, she would be dead set against this marriage; she hated Italians." I was raised to respect my elders, so I didn't say anything. I was furious with a dead woman that I didn't even know.

Despite the fact that I had a ring and we were officially engaged, Brian hadn't asked my father for his blessing. So began the strained love/hate relationship between my future husband and my father. My father, as the head of the family, felt it his duty to advise his children, married or not, but to Brian this appeared old fashioned and unwelcome. In time, he learned to value my father's advice when making important decisions, but initially it was foreign territory.

Erminia, on the other hand, loved Brian. "He's a policeman, so I know he's an honest man. But September is not a good month for a wedding. I was married in September, and I lost your grandfather so young. Your aunt was married in September, and her husband grew sick, leaving her with no money and many children to raise." When Brian had a mild heart attack in August 2001, still a young man, my grandmother's words haunted me.

At a bridal shower thrown by the Kindys, Brian's Aunt Sue was shocked when she met my mother, not an olive-skinned woman dressed in black but a woman with a fair complexion in pastel florals.

At the bridal shower thrown by the George family, I was three hours late as Brian and I had gone to his cousin's cottage for the weekend and had car problems. The food was eaten by the time I arrived, because Fidel's mother had invited half the neighbourhood despite the fact that they had not been invited to the wedding. My mother now felt compelled to send invitations to all of them, with 200 guests already on the list.

The church was very lopsided the day of the wedding: only 50 guests on the groom's side and over 150 on the bride's. Brian's family felt like they were attending a

Broadway production carefully orchestrated by Father Bouvier. After the service we sat down to a roast beef dinner.

My parents wanted spaghetti, but I couldn't eat it on my wedding day after having it three days a week for the better part of my young life. Besides, Sunday was spaghetti day and I was marrying on a Saturday. We compromised and served roast beef with my Uncle Primo's homemade Italian wine. This part of the reception was catered, but my mother prepared an Italian feast for the "late night snack." Tables were laden with pizza, Italian meats and buns, cheeses, salads, fruit, desserts, coffee, and tea. My aunts spent the evening in the kitchen rather than on the dance floor. Brian's family left full and exhausted. They talked for months afterwards about having two dinners. I tried to explain the custom, but soon gave up and just smiled when they spoke of it.

Our children, Paul and Heather, were raised on Italian food and although we didn't eat spaghetti three times a week, we did have it twice weekly. I had to learn to cook, but my mother didn't have recipes. I would be in the middle of cooking something and call my mother to ask "How long do I cook this?" "Cook until done," she would answer.

FUNERAL #1:

REGINA MIRAGLIA GEORGE, OCTOBER 1992,

ST. MARY'S ROMAN CATHOLIC CHURCH, BARRIE, ONTARIO

Regina's heart stopped one cold, snowy morning in October. As the guests slowly dispersed from the cemetery, my brother Bill realized that the funeral directors had placed our mother's casket facing east toward the rising sun, according to standard procedure. Bill knew our mother hated the sun and asked that she face west to view her favourite sunsets. With the help of a few remaining guests he turned the casket. He then wondered if it had been placed properly to begin with and turned it again, then again and again. We left, unsure which way she actually faced, but secure in the knowledge that Regina would watch over our family forever regardless.

WEDDING #3:

HEATHER AND STEVE, AUGUST 1996,

ST. MARY'S ROMAN CATHOLIC CHURCH, BARRIE, ONTARIO

Heather married Steve Reynolds, neither Italian nor Catholic. He proposed during Heather's last year of college just as she was considering extending her studies another three years to attend university. I felt she was too young, but Steve didn't want to wait.

"Just because you get married, doesn't mean you can't go to university," I compromised. She decided to work for a year as a teacher's assistant and take classes part time toward her teacher's degree. Meanwhile, they participated in a weekend retreat with other couples to discuss various aspects of marriage, goals, finances, and children.

At a bridal shower thrown by the Reynolds family, Heather learned that Steve's mother disliked Catholics and his aunt disliked Italians. The aunt, who worked at the Bay, told Heather that an Italian woman had been caught shoplifting. She asked, "Do you know her?"

Heather chose red roses and lily of the valley for her bouquet, like her mother and grandmother had. The choir sang "Ave Maria" as they had for my mother and I. Heather wanted pasta and chicken but we couldn't have chicken because Uncle Domenic didn't eat chicken, so we had roast beef with an additional course of cannelloni. I had everything catered.

Steve was worried that the wedding was going to be "too fancy." He wanted a cash bar; I insisted on an open bar. Steve found himself defending every suggestion at our house. "My family doesn't even talk during dinner," Steve sighed.

WEDDING #4:

PAUL AND DENISE, OCTOBER 2001,

COLLIER STREET UNITED CHURCH, BARRIE, ONTARIO

Paul met Denise, divorced mother of five-year-old Kurtis and neither Italian, nor Catholic. They were engaged just before Christmas and the wedding was planned for October 13th.

Denise had never been baptised so the Catholic church did not recognise her previous marriage; they could have it annulled but it would take over a year and cost a lot of money. Instead they chose to get married in our local United Church, "Ave Maria" and all. Brian and I hosted the reception with a four-course Italian meal, complete with cannelloni and breaded chicken.

"What about Uncle Domenic? He doesn't like chicken," Paul worried.

"It's okay, we'll tell him it's breaded pork." Certain things don't seem to be as important as they once were.

A year after their marriage, Denise gave birth to twin boys — Nicolas and Bryson. Paul chose the Italian spelling of Nicolas. Paul also planted his own garden, growing long green beans from seeds brought over from Italy. He transplanted asparagus and chicory from his grandfather's garden, and grew watermelon and cantaloupe in our cold Barrie climate as his grandfather had taught him.

Heather is expecting her first baby in August. I will cook my grandchildren the Italian foods my mother cooked for me, and I'll watch this next generation grow. Perhaps one day they'll phone and ask, "Grandma, how long do I cook the spaghetti gravy?" and I'll reply, "Cook until done."

Like Pigs to Slaughter

FRANCESCA SCHEMBRI

Venera pulled the linen sheet over her eyes, while her husband checked for proof of her virginity. Satisfied, Giacomino then returned to his side of the bed. Venera's aunt, Vannina, had whispered into her ear before the honeymoon, "Spread your legs and close your eyes. Do whatever he tells you to do, and everything will be fine." Fine? For whom, she wondered. Venera had imagined her wedding night to be the result of courtship and romance and the beginning of a never-ending journey of passion. She had dreamed of leaping into her prince's arms, the air scented with the fragrance of jasmine and orange blossom. After all, she was only 20; she had dreams, she wanted to marry for love.

Peppa, her mother, had other plans for her, which did not include any of this nonsense. Suddenly, Venera found herself in bed with a man she hadn't known until a couple of weeks ago. He was an *americano* returned to his nearby hometown for a month-long vacation and to search for a wife. Venera's father had died a year before the end of the Second World War; because she was an orphan, she did not have a dowry. Venera resented marrying a stranger, but her mother was very clear that at 20 she wasn't likely to find a more suitable husband than Giacomino, who wasn't asking for any dowry, and also was willing to take care of all the expenses. To make things worse, her cousin had had a child while unmarried, and had shamed the entire extended family. The message was clear: she couldn't afford to be choosy.

Giacomino was short, stocky, dark haired, and spoke with a deep voice, avoiding eye contact. When he sat in Venera's one room house, now her official fiancé, he never uttered a loving word to her. Venera couldn't help thinking that he wasn't attracted to her, yet his desiring eyes often fell to her breast when he thought she wasn't looking. Once, while playing cards with the men in the family his hand made its way between Venera's legs; she was confused by this strange behaviour. Meanwhile he continued to bark orders and to offer little more than the merest of greetings.

The morning after their engagement, as it was her duty, Giacomino was introduced to the eldest relatives who were too frail to leave their houses. Walking side-by-side with Giacomino and escorted by her mother, Venera bumped into her best friend's brother who stopped to congratulate her on her good fortune. Giacomino grew suspicious. Once at home, he pushed her inside and angrily implied that she was a whore to even speak with another man in his presence and without his permission. Offended, Venera cried while her mother, drawn to the kitchen by Giacomino's curses, reprimanded her daughter and apologized to him on Venera's behalf. She was told to cease her crying and learn to bear it: "You'll see, it's not so bad. Give him some attention and be a good wife — that's it!"

A meeting was arranged with father Ernestino to inform him about their wedding plans. Promising a large donation to the church, Giacomino told the priest to cut through the red tape and speed up the procedure as he had to return to America in two weeks. The priest told him that the only way this could be accomplished was to marry in the chapel, as if the couple had eloped. Giacomino agreed without consulting Venera. The date was set for the following Thursday afternoon. She had a week to get ready. Another of Venera's dreams fell by the wayside. Since puberty, she had dreamed of wearing a traditional white gown, but it was no longer possible; a woman who eloped and who married in the chapel was not permitted to wear white.

The women in the neighbourhood joined in the preparations for the wedding: relatives, friends, and neighbours passed around swatches of ivory woollen fabric for a two-piece suit. "It would be more appropriate for a bride and useful for future occasions." Venera remained passive and did not take part in the decision-making, If it was not white lace, nothing else mattered. As Giacomino was paying for it, he selected instead a navy blue fabric that could be worn all year round. The fitting of the two-piece dress was an event itself: all the young women in the block were there, admiring Venera's new dress. The dressmaker complimented Peppa on Venera's beautiful figure, "*Ha preso dalla buonanima di suo padre; era alto, veramente un bell'uomo.* She looks like her father;

he was a tall and awe-inspiring man," Peppa replied. Listening to the compliments, Venera felt a sense of loss and a bitter taste lingered on her rosy lips.

While Venera's friends helped her pack they commented on her luck; it was unfair that she was getting *sistemata* (married) and going to America while they were still waiting for their turns. Venera tried to dissociate herself from this new reality. In less than 24 hours her life would change forever: she was marrying a man that had never courted her, talked to her of love, or kissed her.

The day before, her aunt Vannina had asked her if she knew what to expect of the wedding night, but Venera's expression clearly conveyed that she didn't. "Do you know what married couples do? How babies are made?" Venera wasn't too sure. Venera's mother had forbidden her to allow boys to touch or kiss her, to even open the house door to a man when alone. "Your wealth is your virginity," was the only piece of cryptic advice she had received.

The day arrived and while Venera was storing the goods her mother had bought at the market, Peppa was complaining about the extra expense of the wedding dinner. Despite the inopportune timing, Venera blurted out that she had doubts about marrying Giacomino, that she was not in love with him, that she didn't even *like* him. She knew that it was a mistake.

"Do you know what you are saying? Are you are crazy? How dare you talk about love! What does love have to do with it? *Siamo poveri e non abbiamo nessuna scelta.* Beggars can't be choosers!" she said with a slap to Venera's face. Once married, things would change. She must think of her family and help them escape their misfortune. Once she was in America she could bring the others over; their future depended on her. If Venera broke the engagement she would never be able to find another suitable husband; without a dowry and with a reputation for ingratitude, she would be destined to spinsterhood.

Walking toward the church wearing the new suit, new shoes (that were too tight), and carrying the new leather handbag, she couldn't help thinking about the first time she had witnessed her father slaughtering a pig. The animal planted its feet in the mud, crying loudly as it was dragged toward the butcher block. In the evening all enjoyed the feast: the delicious sausages, the pork chops, the wine, music, and dance. Of course it would have being silly to mourn a pig. "The vulnerable must be sacrificed, so that others can live," concluded Venera, walking a little faster.

Adjusting his pace to Venera's, Vannina's husband,

who was to give her away, suggested that the bride was rushing because she couldn't wait to become a wife. Her mother proudly waved to the women who were standing on the street congratulating the bride on her good fortune and said with conviction, "My daughter deserves it."

Food for Thought

ROSANNA BATTIGELLI

Angie absentmindedly moved the handle of the meat grinder a quarter turn.

"I told you I'm not ready yet," her mother exclaimed sharply. "Aren't you listening to me?"

Angie swallowed a retort and watched silently as Francesca fit a pork intestine over the top of the funnel attachment on the meat grinder and tied the end of the casing with string. Occasionally her eyes shifted to the intense face of her mother, noting the shadows and lines, the sagging jowls, the grey, thinning hair.

"Okay, Angela, I'm ready. *Avanti.*"

With her left hand, Angie put the coarsely ground pork meat into the machine, turning the handle slowly with her right hand. She pushed the meat in carefully with her fingertips, avoiding the turning blades.

"Push like this," her mother directed, abruptly moving Angie's hand aside.

"The *salsicce* won't come out good if you don't get all the air out." She pushed down forcefully on the meat in the opening and then returned to her job, pricking the sausage with a needle as it filled the casing, to eliminate trapped air. "Faster, or it will take all day."

"If you wanted a professional sausage maker, you should have hired one," Angie returned, her irritation growing.

"If your father was alive I wouldn't have called you. You never did like this kind of work," came her mother's curt response.

Angie counted to 10 silently. It was almost a year since her father had died, and the mention of him could still elicit tears. She shut her eyes, willing herself to keep her emotions under control. "I didn't like it because I could never do it well enough for you," she said, struggling to keep her voice even. "You should try not to be so negative, Mother," she added dryly.

"Don't start with me. Concentrate on what you're supposed to be doing."

Angie surveyed the container holding the ground meat of four pork shoulders. That job had been done the night before: cutting the meat off the bones, chopping it up into pieces, grinding it coarsely, and finally adding the salt, chili peppers, and fennel. The sight and smell of all that raw meat had made her come close to considering vegetarianism.

This part isn't so bad, she thought, moving her fingers to a silent rhythm, imagining herself in an assembly line. They worked silently, methodically, the only sounds being the churning of the meat passing through the machine and the release of air from the needle pricking the casing. On the counter in the spacious basement kitchen, the old alarm clock kept vigil.

"Where are the kids?" Francesca asked suddenly, startling Angie.

"With their father."

"*Vigliacco.*"

"Ma, there's no need to insult him. We settled our differences."

"You broke up the family," she said bitterly.

"Ma, I explained this to you. He was never home. I thought he would lighten up on work once we got married and had kids, but he never changed. He was a workaholic, Ma. Work first, wife and kids second. He left before the kids woke up and didn't get home until after they were in bed. We couldn't live like that anymore. Well, maybe *he* could, but I couldn't. . . . It was the best for everybody."

"Young people today don't know what's best, or there wouldn't be so many divorces," Francesca spat, pricking the sausage harder. "*Basta!*" she cried suddenly.

Angie stopped turning and watched as Francesca tied the end of the sausage and placed it with the others already coiled on a nearby table, where later she would tie them further to make individual links. Lifting another pork intestine soaking in a bowl, she positioned it on the funnel spout and with a wave of her free hand, signalled Angie to continue.

Francesca may have adopted a new country 40 years ago, Angie mused, but she remained in Italy emotionally. Sure, she had learned English by watching television, but she had preserved most of the old-country traditions, including the double standard that existed for males and females. Angie's brother Vinnie could spend the whole night out with his buddies and Angie couldn't.

"Vincenzo is a man. He can protect himself." Francesca would tell her, when Angie complained about her curfew. "Girls have to be more careful."

Angie was married at 18, lived two blocks away, but still felt like she was under Francesca's thumb. It was her separation five years later that had made her stronger, independent, and confident.

"I need to talk to you about something, Ma." Better to get it over with.

"You need money?" The needle stopped in mid-air and Francesca's piercing black eyes met hers.

"My divorce is final."

"*Che mi dici?* You didn't tell me you were getting a divorce." The words were ominously calm.

"Ma, I tried to talk to you but you never wanted to listen. Every time I brought up anything about the separation, you'd practically cover your ears. I told you John and I weren't getting back together. Did you think I was going to stay separated forever?"

"*Povere creature,*" Francesca exclaimed, shaking her head dolefully from side to side and pursing her lips in an all too familiar manner.

"My children are not poor creatures," Angie shot back. "If this wasn't the best thing for them, do you think I'd be doing it?"

"You're doing it for yourself, not for them," Francesca scoffed, eyes flashing. "If you were thinking about them, you'd keep the family together."

"For better or worse, right, Ma?" Angie's voice was edged with anger. "How can you tell me what's best for them? Did you live with us?"

"You could have given him another chance, for the sake of the children."

Angie's mouth fell open. "Haven't you heard a word I've said? It's over, Ma. Accept it. I'm not here to get your approval or your advice. I *am* an adult. I can make my *own* decisions and deal with the consequences."

"You never wanted to take my advice," Francesca said bitterly. "If you had, you wouldn't be in this mess." Angie's lips parted to respond, but Francesca lifted her hand firmly. "*Basta!* Enough! I have work to do." She fitted a new pork intestine over the spout, tied the end, and picked up the needle. Angie eyed the remaining mounds of ground pork, trying to calculate how much time it would take to finish — 15–20 minutes.

When her father and Nonna were both alive, Angie

would sit on her nonna's knee, munching happily on *torrone* and listening to tales of the yearly pig slaughter in the old country and the tradition of draining the blood from a slit in the pig's neck, then boiling it with milk, pre-fermented wine, cloves, cinnamon, lemon, and orange peel to make blood pudding.

Nonna had been very superstitious. Angie had innocently taken her nonna's black kerchief and tried it on, only to have Nonna whip it off her head and then quickly make the sign of the cross, before lecturing Angie about the *mala fortuna,* the bad luck that would befall her if she wore a black article of clothing, or if she spilled oil (hadn't Domenico Salvatore's mother dropped dead of a heart attack the morning after he had spilled a half litre of oil?), or if she crossed arms with anybody.

"*Ecco!* It's done!"

Angie watched as her mother placed the last sausage link on the table.

"I'll tie them and hang them up later," Francesca told her, wiping her hands on her faded apron.

"I'll help you clean up," Angie heard herself offering, despite her desire to leave.

"No," Francesca replied firmly. "*Basta* for now. I'm tired." She headed up the stairs, her shoulders stooped with weariness. "I made some minestrone last night, like Nonna used to make. It's in the fridge. You want some? I'll warm it up."

Angie followed slowly, her eyes dropping to the shoes her mother was wearing — her father's old slippers. Tears welled in her eyes. She wiped them hastily with her sleeve. In the foyer upstairs, Francesca turned to face her. "Well, are you staying?"

Angie's eyes locked with Francesca's. A moment of indecision passed. Francesca looked away, then began to shuffle toward the kitchen.

"Sure, Ma. Just a small bowl."

Full

LUCIANA RICCIUTELLI

for Stephen Atkinson

When it happened, I knew what my mother must have felt the instant she died. The sound of it, the moment of impact, metal slapping against metal. It was as though the whole thing happened to someone else. I was not in my body, but somewhere just above it, aware of the airbags that had filled the car, aware that my left arm and left breast were burning, aware that my daughter, my baby, was trapped in her car seat behind me. When the car finally stopped, crumpled up against a hydro pole, I jumped out and pulled my daughter to safety. I was numb.

My mother's car slammed into a tractor trailer filled with cows. Her car was crushed beneath its cab, her body was bruised and folded in on itself. The road was icy. She had lost control. The trailer jackknifed into the ditch. The cows mooed, distressed by the impact.

My father arrived a few moments after the police. They tried to hold him back. Her arm was hanging outside the open window, as it had been a thousand times before. We were sure she must have fallen asleep at the wheel. She hung her arm out the window when she was tired, palm pressed against the cold air.

What was she thinking about, I used to wonder, in that second, when the roof of the car came crashing down on her? Once, in her youth, a gypsy in Rome had read her palm. Then the lines in her hands still bore the promise of a future, of a life that could be rosier, better, easier. That gypsy had told her she would die young and my mother had been waiting for her death ever since. Whenever she was angry with us, she would remind us that soon, very soon, she would leave us for good. After awhile we too waited for her death. Maybe, in that second, she knew the gypsy's prophecy had finally come true.

We were not allowed to view her body — "It is in no condition to be seen," the man at the funeral home insisted — and so she remained alive to me in my dreams. For years afterwards I dreamt her death had been her joke on a family that didn't appreciate her, that didn't love her enough, that didn't understand her anger, her pain, her madness.

~

When I was a baby, I used to scream at night. Neither my mother, nor grandmother, nor grandfather, nor father, nor any of the boarders in our home, could soothe me, could stop the crying. I had been cursed. There was no other possible reason for the haunting cries that made them wish that they were back in their village.

My mother and grandmother poured salt on the windowsills outside my bedroom every night to keep the witches from coming into my room. My grandmother prepared a bowl of water she would cradle in her left arm. With her right hand she gingerly tipped a teaspoon of olive oil, turning it ever so slowly to allow two or three drops of the oil to fall into the bowl, all the time muttering under her breath, stopping only to make the sign of the cross several times with her thumb on my tiny forehead. I didn't know it then, but she was praying. If the oil spread through the water, dispersing into many small droplets, she would nod and without saying a word my mother would know that the *maledizione*, or curse, had not been lifted. My grandmother would have to pour the water and oil down the kitchen sink and start the whole process over again.

At last the oil floated on top, one large, shiny pool. The curse had been banished. The screaming finally stopped. The boarders, sleeping two and three to a room, could finally get a good night's rest.

~

I come from a long line of women whose curses bind them together, like the balls and chains clamped around the feet of prisoners, preventing movement and flight, preventing freedom.

When my mother met my father in Rome and decided in a hurried moment that she would marry him and come to Canada, her mother exploded with fury. She had been able to prevent several marriages, but this time my mother could not be swayed. I'm not so sure if it was love or the need to escape.

"I curse you," her mother raged, "so that one day you too will have a daughter who will leave you!" A mother's curse always comes true, my mother added gravely every time she told the story.

My mother's birth parents had been too poor to keep her. She was the last of six children. My grandmother gave birth to her in the fields, squatting behind rows of ripe tomato plants. As an infant, my mother was small, scrawny, and incredibly hungry. It was a hunger she would never be able to satisfy. My grandmother scooped her up and placed her under the shade of a fig tree. There was still work to be done and six other mouths to feed. She would give this hungry, mewling baby to her sister, who lived in Rome, childless and lonely. My mother's aunt raised her as though she were her own, loved her as much as her own flesh, too much maybe. But my mother never forgave her real mother for giving her away, even though she learned to call her aunt Mamma and her uncle Babbo.

When my mother was 12, her real father died. They said it was pneumonia, tuberculosis probably. She hardly knew him. He had never spoken to her, even when she returned to the farm for the occasional Sunday outing. He would stand in the shadow of the shed that housed their chickens, a crumpled hat over his eyes, one leg pulled up, foot resting against the door, a hand in his pocket, the other expertly rolling a bit of tobacco between gnarled and calloused fingers. Once she thought she caught him eyeing her under the brim of his hat, curiously, as though he wasn't sure who she was. But, when her eyes met his, a pale, washed-out blue, he looked away, embarrassed.

Some months before, my mother's aunt and uncle bought her a new coat. It was bright red, her favourite colour. Her older brothers surprised her with a matching red patent purse and shoes. When her father died, the coat, worn but once, was dyed black. The handbag and shoes were exchanged for something more sombre. I have a photograph of my mother, the one time she got to wear the red coat and shoes, the red handbag clasped tightly in her hand. Her lips cannot betray the shy, pleased smile that lurks at their corners, allowing herself to be happy for one, brief moment, content and full.

After my grandfather's death, my grandmother ran the farm by herself. She had grown up on that farm and knew the land better than she knew herself. Neither her brothers, nor her father, had survived the First World War. When her husband died, my grandmother was relieved; she would never be pregnant again.

They say my grandmother went mad after the death of her first-born son. After World War II, he had worked in a munitions factory. One day the factory blew up. No one knew for certain why. When they told her he was dead, she didn't believe it.

"Where's the body?" she asked, calmly smoothing back strands of steel grey hair.

"It was an explosion," the foreman explained, offering her the large and bloodied sheet he held cradled in his arms. "This was all we could find."

She reached for the sheet, and without speaking, counted the pieces. "There's an ear missing," was all she said as she methodically placed each piece of her son's body into a large cardboard box. She went out to look for the missing ear, roaming the fields under the grey cast of moonlight. She was never the same after that. Every night she wandered the fields and hills, restless and despairing. After awhile, the people in the village no longer heard her wails. It was just the wind, they said.

My uncle had been planning to marry a girl from the village. My grandmother had been wild with jealousy and refused to give her blessing. No one was good enough for the son who had survived the war and returned home with a medal. No one was good enough for the son who turned over every penny he made. The day the factory blew up he and my grandmother had argued violently. In a rage, she cursed him, saying he would come home in pieces.

A mother's curse always comes true.

When my mother was 16, she was hired by the richest family in town as a domestic. It was there that she learned to cook. The man of the house, a prominent member of Parliament, liked to watch her make the fettuccine, kneading it, slicing it with skill and precision, her hands and arms dusted with flour, her soft, curly hair, unusually blond, falling into her eyes. His wife found the whole situation irritating and eventually let my mother go. My mother's *babbo* was furious. They depended on the money she earned since he was too sick, too arthritic, too drunk to work. When she told him the news, he beat her black and blue. She took to her bed. She lost weight. Her eyes began to sink into her face. The witches in the village told her mamma that someone had cursed her and that the curse was drawing all the life from her body.

Country air, they were told, would do the trick so she was sent to a small village near Bologna where they had family who worked the fields. She liked being outside, digging her hands into the soft earth of the wheat fields. It didn't take long for them to discover what a good cook she was and soon she was given the privilege of access to the pantry. She was gratified by the way they slurped their soup, the broth's delicate flavour gently coaxed from a small onion, a piece of celery, a carrot, the carcass of a chicken roasted the Sunday before, a tomato plucked from the vine, parsley crushed with minced garlic and the rind of a lemon, a prized egg beaten lightly with cheese.

Not long afterwards, the rich politician in Rome became ill. No one could help him. He was dying, they told her, and, in his stupor, he kept calling her name. Her father came to the village to bring her back to the city. *Il padrone* wanted to see her. When my mother made her way to his room, he took one last look at her, lifting himself from the bed in anticipation of her innocent face, and died. He had been responsible for the curse placed on her; he couldn't die until he saw her one last time. His death meant the curse was finally lifted.

She was not allowed to go back to the village near Bologna. They found her a job embroidering sheets with a neighbouring seamstress; this made it easier for her parents to keep an eye on her.

~

My mother cursed me when I was 17 years old. "May you never be happy one day in your life!" she screeched at me in a fit of anger when I had dared to go on a date, once, and fancied myself in love. I was not allowed to go out, at all. We had gone to a movie. My father had been home but my mother was away. She didn't learn about it until many

weeks later, when my father confessed. She forbade me to
see him again. I refused. *"Putana,"* she hissed, "what has
he done to you that you should choose him over me?"

Her fury was uncontrollable. She pummelled me with
her fists, her arms, her face flushed red-hot, perspiration
streaming down her temples, beading over her lips. This
wasn't the first time, nor the last.

When it was over and she left the room, I crawled into
bed, my body aching. I recited Hail Marys over and over
in my head until, finally, I fell asleep.

I stopped going to high school. My teachers, witnesses
to the bruises, said nothing.

I don't know when I finally stopped praying, stopped
believing.

My mother used to tell me that if she hadn't discovered she was pregnant with me, she would have left
my father. Even in the early days of their marriage, he
was always looking at other women, talking about other
women. Once he told me that when he first moved to
Canada, he rented a basement apartment from an Italian
family. They had a very beautiful daughter. He used to
like watching her climb the stairs so that he could peer
up her dress. He liked telling stories like that. He was a
good-looking man in his younger days and had many
girlfriends. One of them used to phone all the time to tell

my mother about her evenings in bed with my father.

Once, when I was little, I heard my mother scream into the phone, "You want him? Take him! He's yours!"

My mother and father used to argue all night. Their shouts filled the still night air. Sometimes, when she was really angry with my father she crawled into my bed. She liked to curl her body around mine, stroke my hair. In my ear, she would whisper that my father was a horrible man, that she was the only one who could ever truly love me. When I got older, she stopped coming to my bed and slept on the couch instead. She used to fall asleep eating cookies and milk in the dark. There was never enough food to fill her up, even though she spent all day cooking for her family, her friends, her clients, herself. She had turned it into a successful business. But it wasn't enough; she was never full.

∼

It wasn't long before I ran away from home and fulfilled the curse my mother's mamma had hurled at her when she chose to marry my father and come to Canada.

After I left home, my mother tried to kill herself by swallowing a bottle of pills. When they revived her at the hospital, she refused to see anyone but me. The police came to get me in the seedy apartment I was renting not far from my parents' home. When she saw me, she grabbed my hand and told me she had tried to kill herself so that she could lift the curse she had laid on me, trading her life for the life of misery she had wished on me.

It wasn't until many years later, after several years of therapy and long after my mother died, that I remembered what had gone on during those adolescent years. I remembered my fear of falling asleep and the shadowy presence in the doorway, my need to open every window in the house so that I could breathe, my shame when I caught anyone looking at me. Finally I could name and touch my uneasiness, my anticipation of terror, my search for places to hide. The curse, real and unreal, certain and not, lived in these memories.

Now when I look at my daughter and pull her close, drowning in the sweet smell of her hair, nursing her in the hushed stillness of the night, I wonder if my mother felt such tenderness for me.

When I had the accident, I reached for my baby, and I understood how her life had become mine, her breath my breath, the beat of her heart entangled with the throbbing of my own. I thought of my mother, folded in on herself, crumpled under a sheet of collapsed metal.

Once she too had a new life squealing in her arms, the promise of a future, a life that could be protected by sprinkling salt on the windowsills, a life that might have filled her up in a way that her husband and food could not. But was it enough to shatter the power of the curse that shaped her destiny and mine, defined her dreams, my nightmares, haunted her into madness and me into silence? I come from a long line of women who survived the harshness of their lives to ensure a better future for their children, who looked to them for the answers, who used work and food and the promise of another life to fill them up inside. When that, too, wasn't enough, they couldn't let go. And, in not letting go, they tightened the chains that bound them together, a stranglehold that ensured their survival, for a time.

I look at the women I come from, am bound to by culture, by memory, by blood, and know that I am not so different, really, except that I can pull them with me, straining the chains until they snap, breaking the hold of the curse, opening wide doors locked by guilt, fear, and apprehension. I understand now that my mother, and her mother before her, in their living, in their heartache and loss, in their struggle to survive, gave me the key to set them, and myself, free.

I look at my daughter, sleeping peacefully, pushing away from me so that she can stretch out her arms and legs, claiming her space, and I know that she is full.

Figli Maschi! May You Have Many Sons!

ANGELA CAPOZZOLO

"*Sono diventato papà!*"
"*E maschio o femmina?* Is it a boy or a girl?"
"*. . . è nata una femmina.* It's a girl."
"*O no, Zio Clemente . . . io volevo un maschio!* Oh no,
Uncle Clemente, I wanted a boy."
"*Eh Franky, tu volevi un maschio . . . se sapessi quanto*

Io volevo io! Franky, you wanted a boy? If you only knew how much I wanted one!"

And so went the telephone conversation in Neapolitan Italian between my eldest cousin and my father, as he informed the extended family of my birth on that April evening. At least, this is what I have been told. Repeatedly.

Although my parents always told this story as a joke, I never found the humour in it. In fact, as a young child, I asked why my father would have preferred his first-born to be a son. I was never given a clear answer. Over the years, I came up with my own reasons. Perhaps, it was because my father was the youngest of seven sons. Perhaps, he felt a son would ultimately help him build a home in this new and unfamiliar country. Perhaps, he, like so many of his generation, had been conditioned to believe that the cultural ideal was to have *figli maschi.*

However, I did understand that their desire to have a first-born son did not mean that I was unwanted. They doted on me. My mother and father spent countless hours answering my perpetual *perché*, questions about anything and everything. I felt accepted and respected. The toys, and the swimming, skating, piano, and tennis lessons were welcome, but it was the fact that they listened to me that was most comforting. After the birth of my sister, four years later, I think my parents resigned themselves to the idea that this was the hand that God had dealt them; there would be no boys in this family.

As fate would have it, most of our *paesani* and friends had sons. When visiting these relatives and friends, I behaved like a young lady, *una ragazzina per bene.* A simple glare from my parents from across any room was all I needed to step back into line. En route to our visits, the warnings were myriad: "Sit down and behave. Don't worry about what the other kids are doing. Yes, you may take a cookie, but just one! Say hello. Say goodbye. Say please. Say thank you."

Boys did not need to say thank you or please. They did not need to sit and endure hours of adult conversation. They could eat as many cookies as they desired. They could even run around rearranging people's furniture and spill drinks on the broadloom and sofas, and with customary Italian hospitality, my parents would accept this. Thank God for those plastic-covered *divani.*

When my cousins' sons visited, all hell broke loose. By the time they left, and believe me — I was counting the seconds — my bowling set was missing a pin, the shuttle from my badminton set was lodged high in the trees, a ping-pong paddle's handle was missing, my plastic pool was cracked due to repeated collisions from my tricycle, one basement window was broken by a "stray" baseball, and my parents' vegetable plants had been trampled. And worse still, they refused to include me in the games. After all, I was small, and just a girl. Yet, my parents said nothing. *Mantenere la pace,* keeping peace was more important than a little justice. Their parents neither reprimanded their sons nor apologized for their destructive behaviour. I could not understand what was so wonderful about snotty-nosed, uncombed, polyester-clad ruffians. What made boys the favoured progeny?

On another occasion, while visiting family friends, my mother and the hostess were discussing their children's academic achievements. When the hostess began to list her sons' accomplishments, my mother, feeling she, too, could share my accomplishments, mentioned I had straight As.

Lina, the hostess, responded, *"Beh, okay che va bene a scuola, Angela, però mica è necessario la scuola per le femmine?* Sure, it's okay that Angela does well at school, but it's really not that important for a woman."

I sat at the edge of my seat waiting for my mother's rebuttal, but it never came. I felt betrayed.

On another visit, at a neighbour's, I decided to join the fun and play hide-and- seek with the three boys, even though I knew I'd pay for it later. We ran through the house yelling like hooligans. It was great! I finally found the perfect hiding place: under a table in the basement. When I felt a hand on my shoulder, I thought I had been found. It was my father's. With disappointment and anger in his eyes, he whisked me back home, delivering me to Mom.

"Aren't you embarrassed . . . acting like a boy!"

Most boys were allowed to "eat and run" after breakfast, lunch, and dinner. They were not asked to assist in clearing the table, nor in washing the dishes. *Dai, vai a giocare!* After a meal, most mothers would tell their sons to go and play. As time passed, those same young boys who gobbled up their meals and ran away to play, grew up to be young men who inhaled meals delivered to them in front of the television by Mamma. Ask any forty-something Italian-Canadian man to recall the heyday of his youth and he will invariably refer to those lazy Sundays when he rolled out of bed at noon and devoured bowls of *pasta fatta in casa* while lying on the couch and watching back-to-back football games.

Those young boys also grew up to be young men who stumbled home in the wee hours of the morning after a night of partying — no explanation needed. Making their way through the house to their bedrooms, they removed layer after layer of clothing, just as snakes shed their skins. Their trail of clothing would remain undisturbed until morning when Mamma would pick each layer off the floor.

These mammas spent hours ironing their sons' underwear, socks, and jeans; polishing shoes; organizing dressers and closets; making beds; and ironing scores of shirts (only to find them on the floor the next day).

Marrying a "nice Italian boy" meant that an unsuspecting wife would be living with a man who had been coddled all his life. Invariably, problems would arise when the new bride came to understand the tacit expectation that she continue the tradition of her mother-in-law.

When my parents realized that my dates with nice Italian boys were becoming more frequent, they felt it necessary to intervene. They feared that a relationship would distract me from my education. They spent many evenings at the dinner table advising me to avoid serious relationships and to focus on my university studies. Ironically, it was my father who would do most of the talking. He warned me about men. When he would inquire about my suitors, I would be dismissive and say, "Oh, he's just a friend."

In his wisdom, he would admonish, "Friends, friends! *Non lo sai che quello non vuole essere 'friends' con te? Finisci la scuola, piuttosto! Tutti questi anni di studio*

*andranno perduti, adesso che si e' messo questo appresso.
Ricordati, che se non hai una professione, nessuno ti
rispetta, specialmente i maschi.* Don't you know that he
doesn't want to be your friend? First, finish school and
start your career. Remember, if you don't have a
profession, no one will respect you, especially men."

Tradition would have it that once I reached my 20s,
my parents should encourage me to find a husband. They
didn't, but I didn't wait for their permis-sion. In love and
impetuous at heart, I decided to marry, though they
preferred I wait. I was simply too young, they argued.
Armed with two degrees, conferred only a month earlier,
I walked down the aisle at the age of 23.

And so began a marriage like so many others within
the Italian-Canadian community, in which a wife's worth
was measured by her husband's mother.

Scoring high on a mother-in-law's meter is a difficult
endeavour, especially when the one who sets it and the one
being evaluated by it are ideologically miles apart. In my
case, I faced a more serious challenge. I was not used to
cooking, cleaning, and, of course, ironing. Instead of prac-
tising and perfecting these wifely duties prior to marriage,
as my mother-in-law would have expected, I had wasted
many years with school. Nevertheless, I went into marriage
knowing full well that I had better learn, and quickly.

My decision to pursue a graduate degree caused an uproar in my husband's family. "Don't you think that you have studied enough? What will you do with all this education? You now have a husband and a house to tend to." Although my husband would intervene, explaining that things were different now, approval was not given. My mother-in-law fervently believed that I was abandoning my wifely duties.

I failed miserably at the first household inspections.

First, I failed the dust test. "*O, che bella mobilia!* Oh, what lovely furniture," she remarked as she passed her finger across the top of our dresser.

"*C'è tanto spazio nei cassetti!* There is so much space," she would say, as she opened the dresser drawer to see how her son's apparel had been organized.

"*Cosa avete mangiato stasera?*" my mother-in-law asked her son what we had eaten for dinner. He would explain that we had been late in getting home, so we ate out. "*Povero figlio, me lo fa morire di fame — ha lavorato tutto il giorno.* My poor son, she's going to starve him! He has worked all day. . . ."

But, on the ironing test, I scored the lowest. "*Ma guarda, che camicia!* Look how wrinkled your shirt is! *Portami le camicie che le lavo e le stiro, cosi le trovi pronte quando ti servano.* Bring me your shirts and I'll wash and iron them for you." My husband took his dirty shirts to his mother. I succumbed. Defeated, I realized that he expected me to take care of him.

"Can you help me with my suitcase?" he would plead every time he set out on a trip.

"What do you want me to help you with?" I responded, dumbfounded.

"Can you fold these things and put them in? You know how to do it better than I do. It'll only take a few minutes. Come on, don't give me a hard time."

When I explained that I did not have any formal training in packing suitcases, he insisted that I simply did a better job. Why should he waste his time trying? As I folded, I would argue that a woman had no greater inclination to perform these chores, nor more skills, than a man did.

Because of my questioning and my arguing, I was branded the troublesome feminist, the anti-conformist, the rebel without a cause, *una ragazza difficile.*

In the first few years of marriage, I was continually asked by my husband's mamma when I would have children, *"Ma figli non ne vuoi fare?"*

When my husband and I considered starting a family, it became quite apparent that we did not see eye-to-eye. Although I acknowledged that he was far more open-minded than his peers, he still quietly believed that a boy should do "boy things" and a girl should do the rest.

During an animated discussion about our unborn child's education, he mapped out our son's education.

"I'm going to make sure that he goes away to college. He'll travel, so he'll know what's going on in the world."

"And if we have a daughter? I'm sure that you'd want the same for her, to travel and to study abroad."

"Well, I don't know about that. Girls are different. I'd be very nervous if she went away to school."

If courage and determination had anything to do with it, I thought, I would raise my son as I would a daughter. I would do everything within my means to be a mamma who fosters independence and responsibility. I knew that the birth of a daughter would require my husband to change, and I secretly hoped for it. Maybe then he would finally understand his wife.

On August 20, 1996, our first child was born.

To the anxious grandparents in the waiting room, he gleefully announced, "*E' nato! E' nato . . . è un maschio!* It's a boy!"

He turned to me and whispered, "I was really hoping for a boy. I had a feeling it would be a boy."

Almost three decades later, my husband's hopes echoed those of my father.

What Is In a Name?

MARIA CIONI

My parents had wanted a girl so badly they refused to consider any other possibility. It was as though the force of their combined wills, which was formidable, would be sufficient to ensure it. Mother was in her late 30s when she had me. She took comfort in the fact that her doctor was reputed to be one of the best in the city. During her monthly visits she would say, "We have a wonderful eight-year-old boy and now my husband wants a girl. I do as well."

As the birth date grew closer, the doctor retaliated. "If the baby is a boy and he has red hair like mine, I will take him."

A startled look crossed my mother's face. "The baby could have red hair. My mother had carrot red hair," she admitted.

"Well, then, is it a deal?"

"No need. It will be a girl."

A few weeks later, when mother heard my shriek greet the world, she asked, "What is it, doctor?"

"Pink ribbons!" he laughed.

With those happy words, her duty done, she succumbed to the anaesthetic and drifted off, awakening to see her husband sobbing.

News that it was a girl spread like wildfire through the family. My brother, Gary, was nearly nine, but he was too young to visit the hospital. He had begged for a sister so he wrote, "To Mummy and the baby. I love you both. Hurry home," on his handmade card.

Throughout the pregnancy my Italian father and American mother had refused to consider names, thinking that it might jinx the desired outcome. Mummy and "the baby" arrived home a week later.

"What shall we name her?" questioned my brother.

Genesio Claudio Vincio Cioni was my father's name in its full glory. Together the four names paid homage to his family ancestors and to their cultural roots. Arriving in Calgary as a scrawny 16 year old, he had yet to grow into it. Perhaps this was one reason why in his hometown, Antrodoco, everyone had a nickname. These names, in the town dialect, were conferred on both families and individuals. Nicknames were given by friends in the spirit of community and friendship, a sign of acceptance and belonging. They must be original and suitable so it took considerable thought to find the right name — perhaps one with historical, descriptive, or ironic relevance — as it would stay with its owner for life and would likely be shared with a future spouse and family. Though such names might sound cruel, in Antrodoco they were simply descriptors. One boy was called "folded ear" and one of father's friends was called *mezzo metre*. "Half metre" was indeed a short man, but it was his ability to cook well that distinguished him in the community. My father's nickname was *pellaru*, skin of an animal, due to the fact that an uncle was a tanner. Although father felt privileged to have a nickname, it had no relevance in his new country.

How did the name Genesio Cioni sound to the ears of Calgarians in 1923? Two Italian names had become very well known in Calgary at the time. The month before father arrived locals were fascinated by the details of a murder trial held at the courthouse where Emilio Picariello and Florence Lassandro were found guilty of murdering a police officer in British Columbia. They were sentenced to be executed on May 2nd in Fort Saskatchewan. Florence Lassandro was the first woman to be hanged in Canada and both she and her partner were Italian.

A sense of shame rippled through the Italian community in Calgary, as it did elsewhere in western Canada. They shared in the disgrace and guilt of the pair's wrong doing. At work and at school, Italians felt the eyes of others watching them suspiciously.

In this milieu, Genesio determined that a less Italian sounding name might smooth his entry. It was common for children, even those born in Canada, to be given an English name in school. My cousins, born in Calgary in the early 1920s carried their English names throughout their adult lives. Giannina was called Jean; Concetta, Connie; Antonio, Tony; Franco, Frank; and Mageste, John. This duality was accepted, but in my father's era few Italian immigrants anglicized their own names.

I know of only one other immigrant, Sam Ross, who changed his name. He had left Italy as a boy named Salvatore Ucci. Sam was a survivor, a professional gambler and the first person my father encountered when he arrived at the train station in Calgary. This expert poker player, skilled at reading faces, easily recognized a befuddled teenager from Italy. Speaking in Italian, Sam got the details and paid for a taxi to send Genesio to his mother's house. Sam took a liking to him and they became friends. Sam saw the merits of a name that the locals could pronounce and remember.

"Gene" was the name my father chose. He also accepted an English pronunciation of his last name — See-o-nee, rather than Ch-o-nee. There is a Cioni coat of arms; a white lion with a blue diagonal sash. The name, originating in medieval Florence, is a corruption of the Italian meaning "of Giovanni." I am certain that my father knew nothing of heraldry, which perhaps made it easier for him to allow non-Italians to mispronounce his name.

For 29 years my mother, born in North Dakota of German parents, was known as Martha Arndt. She took father's name when they married in 1939. Socially, she observed the custom of the day, and answered to Mrs. Gene Cioni. She of course knew father's Italian name but to her American ear, Mrs. Gene See-o-nee sounded nicer, "much softer." Father anglicized his name, mother Americanized it.

On September 10, 1939, while Gene and Martha were celebrating news that they were expecting a baby in April by attending the Millarville races, the loud speaker announced, "Canada has declared war against Germany!" Consequently, when my brother was born he was named Gary Gene, the Genesio noticeably absent. The desire to keep a low profile if of German or Italian descent, ruled the day.

In June, 1940, Canada declared war on Italy and in August the Canadian government undertook the National Registry of all adults in the country. My parents were now "enemy aliens" required to report regularly to the police station to be watched and tracked. During the war, the Burns Meat Packing plant ran 24 hours a day. Father managed the plant cafeteria and did two shifts a day for nearly two years. He contracted double pneumonia. The rest afforded him time to think about his future.

In the Italian neighbourhood of Riverside, in December, 1948, my father opened the first Italian restaurant in Calgary. It was at 111A 4th Street North East, modestly located in the basement of a large house, owned by a *paesano*. One might think this the perfect occasion to use an Italian name, but father resisted. He called the place GENE'S SPAGHETTI PARLOR. He had made his professional mark as cook and caterer for more than twenty years by that name.

My mother called in the text for the first ad in the *Calgary Herald*. During her married life, she had evolved from a woman who worked into a business woman. She was Martha Cioni, a woman who managed the dining room and the staff of her husband's restaurant, a woman who signed the cheques and kept finances in order.

Martha and Gene flipped through the Wednesday March 2, 1949 edition to find the entertainment listings on page 27. To their horror the announcement read: JEANE'S SPAGHETTI PARLOR. The newspaper transcriber had assumed, incorrectly, that the name in the ad referred to my mother. My father swore and paced and my mother immediately got on the phone to the newspaper. The following week correctly cited GENE'S SPAGHETTI PARLOR and within two weeks the phrases "Real Italian" and "Excellent Italian Cuisine" were added (likely at no cost).

The small basement space created intimacy, aromas circulated, and its reputation grew. Primo Carnero, the famous former World Heavyweight Boxing Champion turned wrestler, was in town and came in to eat on June 23, 1949. Everyone knew Carnero's hard luck story. Making nearly a million dollars during his boxing career in the U.S. from 1928–34, the champ returned to Italy nearly penniless, having been duped by crooked managers. Hardship ensued; he was put in a Nazi slave labour camp then escaped to join the Italian underground. The successes and tragedies of his life were a drama the public, Italians in particular, followed closely. So popular was his story that it was made into a movie, *The Harder They Fall*, in 1956, with Humphrey Bogart.

The six foot six inch Carnero folded his body to squeeze through the entrance and was greeted in Italian by my father, eager to shake the famous hand. The neighbourhood was in a frenzy, and people flocked to see him on the big night.

Gene telephoned his nephew. "Nino, come quick and bring the camera. Carnero is here!"

Minutes later the veteran army photographer entered and began shooting as the handsome celebrity stood in front of the stove, his impressive frame nearly touching the ceiling. Dressed in a light suit, dark shirt and multicolour tie, he held one hand of the small cook whose white cap brought him to the champion's shoulder. Others lined up to record their brush with greatness. Ivo

Brandelli, who lived in the apartment above the restaurant, was next. Slimmer than father and without the height advantage of the cook's hat, the illusion was Lilliputian.

Gene's reputation was spreading among his customers (there were no restaurant critics at the time). In a city of just over a 100,000 people, word travelled fast. A *paesano*, the landlord, offered father a partnership that would have him move next door to a much larger space. The agreement was sealed with a handshake. Gene's Spaghetti Dine and Dance opened on New Year's Eve, 1949. Business boomed and the good times lasted for nearly two years until father realized that his partner was taking financial advantage. The friendship was over and Gene walked away. "I'll go elsewhere and start again," he declared.

"Go, but this is the only Gene's!" his partner uttered in a parting shot.

My mother wouldn't give up without a fight. "You have given your life, your family, to build your name and you have succeeded. Your name is all that you have. We will hire the best lawyer in town."

At the consultation the lawyer came to the point. "What do you want?"

"I want my name. I will move on, open another restaurant, but I must have my name."

Father opened his third restaurant, La Villa, in mid-April, 1952. Mother managed to work his name into the newspaper advertisement four times. The former partner knew that he needed Gene's name to attract customers so he placed an ad in the Saturday newspaper a couple weeks later, reading: "There is only *one* GENE'S DINE & DANCE in Calgary . . ."

While some patrons were baffled, others were amused. Just one dinner at the old restaurant and the patrons immediately knew that Gene Cioni was no longer in the kitchen. He wasn't making his rounds in the dining room.

"Gene is off tonight," was a standard reply, but with word of the new restaurant circulating quickly, supporters soon found La Villa and regaled Gene with news of these excuses.

In August Gene placed his photo in the La Villa advertisement. There, in a formal white chef's hat and bow tie, a smiling Gene Cioni, originator of Calgary's Italian cuisine, left no question as to his whereabouts. It was only a matter of time before the charade ended. In December, 1953, the former partner renamed his restaurant The Isle of Capri.

People have a way of growing into their names — Gene had finally grown into his. Now it was my turn.

"Lana! The baby should be named after Lana Turner, my favourite movie star!" declared my mother home from the hospital.

"I would like to call her Maria in honour of the Madonna of the Grotto in Antrodoco," my father said. Pride in his Italian heritage no longer carried the fear of reprisal. Times had changed.

Italian by Choice

CARRIE-ANN SMITH

Two of my great-aunts, Mary and Theresa, were walking down the hallway of a Las Vegas hotel when they passed a handsome, dark-haired young man who gave them a big smile. "Must be an Italian boy from the Sault," one said to the other. "He looked familiar. I'm sure I have seen him around the neighbourhood." It was Sylvester Stallone. True story.

I grew up in the warm centre of a ravioli universe. I couldn't speak Italian, but I possessed a few choice curse words. I knew the names of all the pastas and the pastries. I thought that every single one of my relatives was Italian and in my mind the world revolved around us. It wasn't a very big world, but it did belong to this strangely pale Italian girl growing up in Sault Ste. Marie, Ontario.

I remember coming home from school and telling my mother that an Italian boy in my class had a phone number that started with 949, and that since ours also started with 949, that all Italian people must have phone numbers starting with 949. After all, we had to stick together, we who were teased for having nonnas and nonnos instead of grandmothers and grandfathers, we who grew up eating under paintings of *The Last Supper* and secretly suspected that it somehow inspired our mothers to prepare six meals a day, we who knew what it was to be paralyzed by the *malocchio* when our parents weren't even in the room.

We were the proud but not the few; Sault Ste. Marie might have had a French name, but it was an Italian town. You can imagine how devastating it was to realize as a teenager that I was only one quarter Italian. A measly 25 per cent; I didn't even have a good half. Despite the obvious — Smith isn't exactly an Italian name — it hadn't occurred to me. However, when I thought about it there was sufficient evidence to support this break-through: we didn't have a kitchen in our basement; our house wasn't in the predominantly Italian West End; and cruellest of all, my mother made spaghetti sauce from a can — the less said the better. On the heels of this revelation came another: this meant that our beloved nonna, Mary Helen Artuso, was not Italian — not half, not even one quarter. She was less Italian than me! Had the world gone mad?

My mother, Theresa Marina Artuso, was the only child of a first-generation Italian-Canadian man from a large family. Marino Artuso and his Dutch-English wife Mary Helen raised my mother in the bosom of his extended Italian family in the Sault's West End. The handsome, mandolin-playing Marino who I have seen only in photographs, once took his daughter to visit a friend who had just bought a new car. Hand in hand they stood looking at the shiny car when my mother said to the proud new owner, "It is a nice car, but is it paid for?" Her words were immediately followed by a bone crushing hand squeeze from her father and "the look." Now, she had heard her father say the same thing a hundred times because Marino never owned a car he didn't pay cash for, but it was not for him to comment on the practices of others. Marino taught Theresa and she taught us; work hard, keep your mouth shut until you get home (or at least in the car), and don't say anything stupid when you are holding the hand of a reasonable adult.

When she was 13, Theresa asked him for a lawnmower to make the straw that grew around their modest house look like grass. He told her that he would pay for half of it, so she saved her babysitting money. Once the lawnmower was purchased she considered the task of maintaining the yard an honour. Imagine telling this woman that you don't want to clean your room. . . .

If I was confused about my Italian heritage, I came by it honestly. My mother's elementary school encouraged the children to wear the traditional dress of their culture at pageants. The eastern European girls, recently arrived in the post-war wave of immigration, would don beautifully embroidered dresses with colourful ribbons in their braided hair. My mother would, without fail, dress like a gypsy. For some reason she believed that this was the national costume of Italy, so, jewelled, sequinned, and clutching a tambourine, she marched off to Catholic school. I blame these cultural theme days for what developed into a lifelong fascination with scarves, big earrings, and all things shiny. She did, however, eventually give up drawing a mole on her right cheek in the 1960s, for which we are all grateful.

Marino died before my siblings and I were born, but our mother kept him alive for us. After she lost her beloved father, she made the first of two interesting matrimonial choices that both ended in divorce, leaving myself and my two siblings to be raised by our mother and "her people." We were surrounded by love, Catholicism, food, and all things Italian. So it was that three pale, fair-haired kids with Anglo names succumbed to an identity crisis.

My little brother wore a "Kiss Me, I'm Italian" sweatshirt until it was threadbare. He is wearing it in almost every photograph taken in the late '70s and early '80s. I remember him wearing it while rollerskating at Wheelies to Joe Dolce's "Shaddap-a You Face." Ah, 1981. It wasn't a great song, and in today's climate of political correctness it is probably considered offensive, but it was Italian and that made it good. In addition to being a roller rink hit, it gave us a new expression. We weren't allowed to use it, but if we happened to be singing the song, and our voices went up at the chorus, it was clearly not our fault.

Every culture has unique expressions, but we picked up a few from my mother that I have never heard anywhere else. I doubt either Italy or Canada would be especially proud to claim credit. One was employed to describe someone who was lazy or less than helpful, the oft heard "ornament of goat shit" — as in, "Quit standing there like an ornament of goat shit." The Italians are a hard working people, so the accusation of impersonating goat shit was powerful. In the category of insults beginning with the words "Quit standing there like" is "Quit standing there like Joe Palooka." I was well into my 20s before I found out that Joe Palooka was not a lazy man from the old neighbourhood.

In addition to being hard working, the Italians are a stylish people. If you made a bold fashion choice in my house you were inviting the observation that you looked like "Nelly from the pickle factory." Nelly isn't even an Italian name; was it "Netta from the winery" in the old country or did my mother just make it up? Are there actually pickle factories where badly dressed girls gather? It sounds sort of Dickensian — best to change clothes.

One thing that we know our mother legitimately inherited from her father was the tendency to talk with her hands. My mother elevated it to an art form best observed from the safety of our nonna's car. On weekends spent at the lake the dreaded ritual of packing the cars was a fate worse than death, during which my brother would invariably break out his impersonation of "an ornament of goat shit." My sister and I did not have to hear a word to know that he was catching hell in the car in front of us, because our mother's hands were flying. In addition to the gestures and obscure expressions my mother employed was the all-purpose code word "English," a magic sword that became a higher form of profanity. I will translate.

"How was dinner at your friend's house?"

"English." (Tasteless and not enough.)

"What do you think of your son's new girlfriend?"

"English." (Skinny and she doesn't help with the dishes.)

"I am sorry your neighbour died. How was the funeral service?"

"English." (No one sang, no one cried, no one brought food.)

Family, food, and church went together as they do in many cultures, but it is the little variations that make them unique. Praying for good weather is not distinctly Italian. Standing in the middle of your office, late for a business meeting, praying out loud to Saint Anthony in order to find your daytimer, is. A first communion party is not distinctly Italian. A first communion party for 50 relatives with three courses and the priest coming over to bless your gifts, is. Making your first confession is not distinctly Italian. Confessing to impure thoughts about Danny Armatullo on *Fame*, well, that's just strange and not to be blamed on my mother or the Italian people.

A few years later my ravioli universe started to feel a little small, so I figured that I would take a look around the old world; the world Marino's people had left behind so long ago. With almost no money and (as I found) not enough Italian profanity, I headed to Europe. During my first night in Rome, I got locked out of the hostel because I had met an American boy and stayed out past curfew. Once the novelty of watching cats sitting on the roofs of cars and playing "What's that Thing Floating in the River" wore off, we decided to check out the Olympic Stadium. The stadium was lined with towering Romanesque sculptures of athletes from a variety of events; God-like figures clutching discs and javelins and the like. That was what I had come to Europe for; this was the old world Italy of my imagination. Then, at the far end of the stadium, I saw Him; a barbarian who had stormed the gates and now stood shoulder to shoulder with half-naked wrestlers and runners from the classical era. I stood in awe, suddenly incredibly homesick, staring up at the stone face of a hockey goalie, who was, without a doubt, Canadian like me.

A few years later, I was at the Canadian Pavilion of the 1992 World's Fair. There was a colossal crowd waiting to gain admittance, so to keep us entertained we were shown a film of Canadian landscapes and faces, set to cheesy music. It was hokey stuff, ripe for derision, which I was just about to voice when I was suddenly enveloped by the theme from Hockey Night in Canada, and I, a sophisticated, intelligent woman on her second trip to Europe, bawled like a baby. It was definitely time to go home.

In 1995, Algoma Steel decided to hire university students to work in the plant. From the first day on the floor of the Plate and Strip Mill I felt like I was communing with Marino and his contemporaries. Due to the recession and mass layoffs of the '80s the average age of steel workers seemed to be about 50, and most of them seemed to be Italian. In the beginning, I was the only girl on my crew and my job was to direct the crane operator. The unofficial but common title for this particular job was "hooker." My first thought was how daring that was going to look on my résumé: a hooker in a steel plant. It wasn't even lunchtime on day one when I sliced my knee on a piece of steel. My colleagues made me see the nurse once the blood reached the top of my steel-toed boot. During my examination the nurse remarked that she had never seen a steel worker with a belly button ring; I was fitting right in. These were my people and there I was, bleeding, bejewelled, and a living, breathing cautionary tale. I was in the first batch of students placed in the mills. Hundreds followed. Somehow the legend of my injury reached every last one of them, growing in severity with each retelling.

Our grandfatherly Italian co-workers brought us vegetables from their gardens, told us stories about the old days, and taught us a few Italian words. I started introducing myself by saying, "I'm Carrie-Ann Smith, but my mother is an Artuso." Sometimes the person I was meeting would know the name and would tell me which of my relatives they had worked with; sometimes they looked behind me for "the special bus" and said, "Aren't you the hooker with the prosthetic leg?"

Once you get a handle like that, you find out who your friends are and you learn to stick together. We 949ers, we who know that if we fly home for a visit our carry-on luggage for the return trip is going to be a giant tub of meatballs. We who explain all the racial slurs on *The Sopranos* to non-Italian friends. We who hear our mother's words coming out of our mouths and blush a little bit less with every passing year. We are the descendants of saints and gypsies, brave souls who populated big cities and small steel towns, logged, mined, farmed, laid railway tracks, built a country. All we have to do in return is be happy, and remember. So we tell our stories and we become that which we love.

Bellosguardo

ANGELA CAPOZZOLO

For my father, Clemente Capozzolo, 1933-2004

In July 1977 at the age of nine, and after months of anticipation, I was about to cross the Atlantic for Fiumicino, Italy. As we neared the airport runway, I peered out the window at the yellow grass — so disappointing compared to the plush green that we had left behind nine hours earlier. Everything looked dry, arid, unkempt. The plane's wheels hit the ground. I surveyed the neighbouring passengers, who made the sign of the cross and burst into a congratulatory applause.

Inside the airport armed officers guarded the customs gates and baggage pickup. I had never seen a gun before and wondered at the need for such security. One of my father's brothers, Zio Peppe, who was a *carabiniere*, entered the arrival area, retrieved our luggage, and quickly whisked us past fellow passengers — fatigued, waiting, and envious — and out onto the crowded street. We skipped all the official checkpoints with a mere flash of a state identification card. Zio Peppe loaded our luggage and we boarded Zio Luigi's Fiat set to take us to his seaside home in Torvaianica, half an hour south of Fiumicino.

The heat was unbearable. There was no air conditioning, and the cramped seating coupled with the jerking manual gears made me long for our Delta '88 Oldsmobile.

We were greeted by three sets of aunts and uncles and eight cousins, each of whom kissed and embraced us in an awkward moment of forced familiarity. Until now, these people had merely been characters in my parents' stories.

Zio Luigi's home was spacious and comfortable,

though without air conditioning. *"Fa male! Ti fa venire il torci collo, o ti prendi un colpo d'aria.* We don't have such unnatural things here," my aunt said. "Anyway, with air conditioning you'll get a cold, or worse still, a stiff neck." The latter was enough to warrant a day off from school or work.

Everything here seemed diminutive: cars, homes, appliances, and beds. Washrooms, however, were spacious enough for a toilet and bidet. "What the heck is a bidet?" I asked my mother. Her explanation was incomprehensible. The washrooms had shower heads, but no shower stall, no bathtub, and definitely no shower curtain. After each shower my mother mopped the flooded bathroom. My aunt admonished, "Shower, shower, *ma perche' te lo fai ogni mattina?"* I had a feeling this daily ritual would be rationed to two or three times a week. When I did not concede, my zia turned off the water heater, leaving me with a soapy head and frigid water. I decided I did not particularly like this zia.

We visited St. Peter's Square, the Sistine Chapel, every famous piazza and fountain in Rome, and of course, the Coliseum, from which I furtively chipped away a stone as a memento. But the highlight of that excursion was gelato. At the *gelateria,* they did not have scoops like ours, but flat, spatula-like utensils with which to pile the smooth gelato into a cup or onto a cone. The selection was incredible. Finally, I picked *cioccolato e nocciola*. What made this the most unforgettable gelato was the warm *panna* they added as a finale. Who would have imagined that it could get any better than Baskin Robbin's Jamoca Almond Fudge?

A couple of weeks later, we left Rome and made our way to my parents' hometown, Bellosguardo (literally, "beautiful view") in the province of Salerno. By "made our way" I mean that on a hot, lazy, Sunday afternoon we negotiated the winding one-lane coastal road up steep cliffs without guard rails. My uncle was forced to stop a few times during the voyage to relieve his car sickness. From the city of Salerno we had to travel inland to Bellosguardo. After an unfortunate emergency stop near Paestum's sulfur springs, we resumed the Formula One-like driving and I prayed that Bellosguardo was worth the painful journey.

We passed the adjacent town, Rocca Daspide, and then started our ascent, spiralling 500 metres above sea level to our final destination. The homes were centuries old, the main roads lined with cobblestones. Inquisitive locals peered out of the windows and doors that lined the main street, intuitively knowing we were new to the town. They exercised no discretion as they called from one window to another, *"E chi sono questi?"* Those up to date with current events quickly relayed the news reporting, *"E' la figlia di Mast'Aniello e il figlio del Bianco — vengono dell'america.* It's Master Aniello's daughter and the son of the White." Master Aniello was my fair-skinned, blonde, and blue-eyed paternal grandfather, who was the master shoemaker .

En route to my mother's childhood home, now the residence of my widowed grandmother, people approached the car. Villagers recognized my parents and wished to welcome them home. They peered into the back seat scrutinizing our faces before coming to the conclusion that my sister Daniela was a replica of my mother, while I looked like my father, who in turn looked like his mother and my namesake, Angelina.

My grandmother stood at her front door, a tall, robust woman with long greying hair she kept in a bun. She embraced my mother and father and gave my sister and me awkward kisses — it was the first time we had met. Nonna knew we had arrived despite the fact that she had no telephone. Word of mouth meant nimble feet made their way through the labyrinth of ancient streets and alleys, by means far more expedient than technology.

We met my mother's two sisters, Silvia and Pupetta. The latter's name was actually Constantina. She had been nicknamed Pupetta, or doll, as a child, and continued to be known by this name. My cousins Rosario (my age) and Fiorenzo (my sister's age) cast suspicious glances our way. Our uncles, Pinuccio, whose actual name was Giuseppe, and Vituccio, whose actual name was Vito, welcomed us as well, but the awkwardness continued. I found it curious how Italians infantilized themselves by adding suffixes like *etta* or *uccio* to their names.

My mother's eyes were wild with excitement as she spoke with her sisters, frantically trying to make up for her 11-year absence. I had never seen her like this; she had friends in Toronto, but no immediate family. I realized how hard it must have been for her to live thousands of miles away from them when I took my own parents and sister for granted.

After dinner, my father took us to his childhood home, a home he wanted to purchase when all five of his brothers wanted to sell it. It was a point of contention and he eventually relented, unable to afford the expense while carrying two mortgages on our house in Toronto. His brothers thought him overly sensitive to want to hold onto the memories of his youth and of his parents when it was so impractical.

My father was quiet as we approached the large front doors. He asked the current tenants if he could show his daughters his childhood home. His eyes were full of tears as he took us from room to room, relating 25 years of memories. As we were leaving, a woman from across the road came to say hello, one of many who had pined for my father.

We were stopped every few feet by people who came out of their homes to greet us and invite us in. We passed a bar where my father was hugged and kissed and our cheeks were pinched. Why did Italians consider this an endearing gesture or sign of affection?

In the following days my mother introduced me to her teacher, Michele Pepe. After my mother had completed Grade 8, *terza media*, he had made a special trip to my mother's home in an attempt to encourage my grandparents to send her to high school in a neighbouring town. She had been top of the class.

I also met my father's frenetic childhood friend, affectionately known as Gambacorta, who, as one of many childhood stunts, had climbed the church tower and sounded the bells in the middle of the night, forcing young and old out of bed. I also met Aristide, my father's deaf-mute friend and barber.

We visited the farmhouse outside Bellosguardo where my father and his family had fled in 1944. From the window overlooking a river, I could see the remains of a bridge that had been bombed by the retreating Germans as they fled American forces. Many American soldiers perished in the village. I had heard my father tell this story at the dinner table on more than one occasion.

I visited my father's family land, affectionately named L'Ischia, and sat under the same ancient oak that had provided my father shade decades earlier.

I had never seen my father's eyes so alive. My parents had seemed so serious and reserved at home, but this new outlook worked to our benefit by offering a new-found freedom we had never experienced in Toronto. We played with neighbouring children, we explored the narrow streets of Bellosguardo with our cousins, we fell upon "haunted houses" like the one owned by *la matta* (the cross-eyed lady), we visited the well where an adulterous woman was drowned by her shamed husband, we played soccer and tennis in the schoolyard, we visited the crowded cemetery where I learned of previous generations of Capozzolos, we visited Chiesa San Michele Arcangelo where my parents had been baptized, confirmed, and married, and we visited the school where my father had enjoyed hours of "heat-free" lessons in the winter months and had knelt in the corner holding two bricks in each hand, arms outstretched high above his head when he failed to complete his homework.

I felt like a student wandering a museum. We set out on these adventures in the afternoon heat, after *pranzo*, despite my grandmother's pleas that we should rest indoors or risk getting sunstroke. We preferred this time of day because young and old had retired to bedrooms for a *siesta*. Between one o'clock and four, Bellosguardo was abandoned. Our youthful voices were the only noise that resounded in the ancient streets and secret passages. Window shutters, *le persiane*, were tightly shut to keep the heat, dust, and bugs at bay.

I practised my Italian. It was an intensive summer language program. When we didn't want others to understand, my sister and I would switch to English. The town's children and teens gravitated toward us since we were a novelty — *le straniere*, the foreigners. But, when they called us *americane*, I became indignant. I corrected them, stating that we were *canadese*. "*E la stessa cosa*," they would say, but it was not the same thing. That year in school we had prepared for Canada's 110th birthday so patriotic fervour was at a peak.

During one of Bellosguardo's many *feste*, I was invited to sing something in English because my uncle was on the organizing committee. I prepared "Canada: One Little, Two Little, Three Little Canadians," a song we had learned at school. I approached the microphone and looked out upon the sea of baffled faces. I froze. Needless to say, I had a short singing career.

What I liked best were our *passegiate*, post-dinner promenades on the main avenue, Strada San Giovanni. Everyone wore their best attire and walked hand-in-hand, or arm-in-arm (even the men), up and down San Giovanni, pausing every so often to accommodate animated discussion, raised voices, and waving hands. The young walked together, teasing, laughing, flirting. It was the perfect forum for acquaintances to be made, friendships to be forged, and young loves to blossom. Every day, I counted down the seconds to the *passegiata*, planned my outfits carefully, sprayed on my aunt's perfume, and expeditiously made my way up the hill to the main road. Women and girls walked ahead of the men in a gesture of gallantry.

When we weren't walking or visiting, we were eating. I don't know how we did not put on weight. We ate, and ate, and ate. I averaged two gelati a day — one at *pranzo* and one on my nightly *passegiata*. *Pranzo*, lunch, was the main course of the day — the meal when everyone returned home from school or work. It consisted of *l'antipasto, il primo, il secondo, e il dessert*. My favourite antipasto was *l'insalata Caprese* made with *mozzarella di buffala*. I enjoyed pasta in every shape and form, *fighi* (black and white figs), *datteri* (dates), *fighi d'India* (prickly pears), *nespole* (medlar). I was tricked into having *cignale* (boar), *anguilla* (eel), *rana* (frog legs), *coniglio* (rabbit), and, almost, *tripa* (tripe). I saw almond, olive, and lemon trees. I even tried *limoncello*. "It's okay, it's homemade. *E' genuine — fatto in casa.*"

For *colazione*, breakfast, we had *caffé e latte* with *fette abbiscottate e cornetti*, toast or croissants spread with cherry or apricot jam, *marmelata di amarena o albicocca*. My grandmother had her pantry, *la dispensa*, filled with milk containers that did not need to be refrigerated! They were triangular prisms resembling the Lola frozen juices back home. I escaped its unappetizing taste and texture by running to my Aunt Silvia's *generi alimentare*, a small grocery story where I could drink real milk and indulge in a selection of treats.

My parents decided to spend *dieci giorni al mare*, ten days at the beach in the area of Paestum and Agropoli, a welcome respite from Glen Long Public Pool in Toronto and the sandy shores of Lake Simcoe and Nottawasaga Bay. Little did I know that we were actually on the prestigious shores of the Amalfi Coast. We stayed at Pensione Santa Lucia, a small, family-run hotel known for its superb meals. The room was small — a double bed for my parents and a bunk bed for my sister and me, the washroom shared with the rest of the guests on our floor. Every morning, we'd wake up, put on our *costumi da bagno*, have *colazione*, and walk through *la pineta* to *la spiaggia*. Once at the beach, my parents would rent *le sdraie e un'ombrellone*, lounge chairs and a cabana. Nothing is "included" in Italy — package deals do not exist.

The sea was spectacular. I stayed in the salty water for hours, ignoring my mother's warnings that I would get sunstroke, *"Esci, che ti viene un insolazione!"* I collected seashells, listened to the waves hit the shore, made castles of all shapes and sizes, and watched the *italiani*. Thin, fat, short, tall, hairy or not, they wore the tiniest of bathing suits. One-piece bathing suits in Italy meant just that — one piece, the bottom part. No one, not even my parents, seemed to care. Some nearby Italian children sculpted a naked couple in sand, complete with strategically placed seaweed. Had this been Wasaga Beach or Jackson's Point, these kids would have been charged with indecency. It was 10 days of heaven.

Like all good things, our trip came to an end. The night before we left Italy, we stayed at my uncle's apartment in Rome. The next morning, after a tearful goodbye, Zio Peppe, with a quick flash of his I.D., escorted us onto the runway tarmac. We boarded the plane and spent the next nine hours in virtual silence.

I wasn't the Angela of six weeks earlier. My frame of reference had expanded. I had experienced the settings and had met the characters in my parents' stories. I had been exposed to a different lifestyle where time was not the adversary. In fact, in Italy, time waited for people while they enjoyed animated, uninhibited discussion, culinary delights, strolls with no particular destination, breathtaking landscapes, spectacular ancient structures, and loved ones. I had tasted my history. I had touched my roots.

When I boarded the school bus to start Grade 4, I was more confident and outgoing. I had renewed respect for my Italian class, where all of a sudden, everything *la maestra* said made sense. I quickly became the top student. When lunch arrived, I was not ashamed of taking out my *panino con prosciutto cotto e bocconcini* from my lunch bag. I never begged my mother for peanut butter and jam sandwiches again. And, most importantly, on Parent-Teacher Night, my parents' Italian accent did not cause me any grief.

I had a new view of the world and it was beautiful.

Riding the Rails

IVANA BARBIERI

AUGUST 15, 1985

"Aqua minerale, café, aranciata, Coca-Cola . . ." I am awakened by refreshment vendors in Napoli Centrale. We've weathered Worldways' non-stop service from Toronto to Ciampino and two hours on a cramped pre-WWII *cabina* I'm sharing with my mother, sisters, and

aunt. Zio Franco, aptly nicknamed The Priest for his teenage years in the seminary, has travelled to Rome to collect us. No Coliseum or Piazza di Spagna for us. After bribing the one-eyed customs agent with 5,000 lire, a value pack of Dentyne, and a carton of Winstons for his trouble, we head directly to Roma Termini.

Zio manages to find us a rail car *"di l'anno di Cristo"* and we settle in for the night. My mother, sister, aunt, and I hog the seats and Zio is left to crash on the floor. Serves us right for travelling on Ferragosto.

SEPTEMBER 3, 1985

I lock eyes with a Sicilian sailor while our train braces for the ferry crossing at Messina Maritima. After three weeks in Calabria I learn there are no limits to stare-offs in this country. My sister and I have let up on *u ciuciu*, Calabria's version of the old maid. He's on the opposite train, likely on leave from the military and making his way down "the boot" for the weekend. Our timing is perfect for the gypsy beggars, spinning tales of the ravages of fire and leprosy. One even carries photos of her kids, *sans* limbs. I'm sickened, but am not breaking my stare. My mother is not convinced and whisks the *zingari* away with a flourish of the hands and *"Vai via!"* After crossing the Straits of Messina, our ship pulls into the harbour; *il marinero* blows me a kiss and I coyly wave goodbye. I scribble my name on the ship rails to remember my first crossing.

SEPTEMBER 11, 1985
We've done our time in Calabria. Nonna is bedridden and I never want to see a stack of cards again. After her sister's fruitless attempts at banishing with the *malocchio*, my mother sneaks me an aspirin for menstrual cramps. The Priest decides it's time for a little culture. All roads do lead to Rome, even from Potame. I would never have believed it possible to visit every-single-site in the Eternal City in 12 hours, but in those days we knew the value of 1,000 lire.

JUNE 1996
I am rewarding myself with a trip to the old country. My obviously Anglo-Saxon friend Jen is dubbed The German. We stay at the cheapest fleabags listed in *Let's Go Europe*. I can live with the tangerine-coloured bedspreads of Sweet Hôtel Plaisance, but by the time we reach Nice we are convinced that the toilet should not be *in* the stall and that a shower curtain a bathroom door does not make. In a massive rush to get to Barcelona (no pain, no gain, no Spain) and *stupidly* ditching the bullet TGV, we

soon find out that if the French trains are relics, the Spanish Talgos are pre-Cambrian. We tolerate sweaty and stinky Dutch campers with sausage lips, flip-flops, and obvious staring problems. Our Talgo yawns to a stop 25 metres from the Port Bou border crossing and sits on the tracks for five hours, baking in the glory of the Spanish siesta. *Viva España!*

Enter Flavio. Jen says I flirt wildly with him, but I think I need to bond with my countrymen after a week with The German. He has just returned from his sojourn in Portugal where I learn you should never wear a *canotiera* for fear of being thought *frosh*. I hear all about the love of his life and he kindly tolerates my dribble about the football oaf I think I am dating back home. We all board the return trip to Nice and share a cabin with an African "Gucci" pedlar. Flavio and I cuddle all the way to Nice. "*Buon viaggio. Belle cose,*" he whispers.

I can't wait to get to Italy! It's been 11 years since my first trip, but I know the land of Dante and Boccacio is in my veins. Everything about the Côte d'Azur changes when we cross into Ventimiglia. Busted sidewalks and laundry hanging out the windows are reminiscent of Zia's first apartment on College Street, but not quite. First stop: *Controllo di Passaporti.*

Jen saunters easily through line. A *carabiniero* stops

me with a baton in the gut. Ugh.

"Passaporto. Cittadinanza," he barks as Jen waves to me from the other side of the customs wicket.

"Italiana," I say.

He adds insult to injury. "Passport." English for the *immigrati*. I watch Jen howl as I struggle with my MEC pack loaded with Chicklets and contraband tobacco.

On the train to Venice we meet Fiore, a judge from Salerno. He talks non-stop for three full hours and tells us that Padua is *bellina* and that Mestre is *brutta*, but a bargain compared to Venetian hostel rates. We marvel at the masterpieces of the Guggenheim and eat the finest pasta in the world.

In Florence Jen and I haggle with the best leather merchants Santa Maria Maggiore has to offer as long as we promise not to squeal to the *Japonesi* or *Koreani* who are *ricchi e rimbambitti* what we really paid. We pull a deal-and-dash at the hostel on the seventh floor and move to its equally dumpy but cheaper cousin on the fifth floor. In five days our host Sandro never cleans our room, turns our underwear blue, and names his *pensione* Nella, short for *Putanella* — little slut — after his charming Yorkshire terrier. What can I say? We could see the Duomo from our window.

Rome has changed in 11 years. I have a bout of lunacy

from the heat in Ostia Antica, am prepared to meet my maker on a death climb through the seven hills, and wear my day pack front style through Porta Portese and the *mercato* of ill-gotten gains in Piazza Vittorio. I bid farewell to Jen in Termini and board my Intercity train for Sicily.

Having paid my dues on those ridiculous flip seats, I reserve my *poltrona*. I have witnessed far too many nonnas having to relinquish their resting spot to reserved paying passengers. I prepare for the changes I know will unfold as we snake southward into the deep-Alabama south that is my legacy. In the toilet I am slightly mortified at the sight of my urine splashing the rail lines and use three wet wipes to scrub and polish my hands before settling in for the six-hour trek to Villa San Giovanni.

The curly haired *ragazzo* I am sharing my rail car with smiles every time I take a picture or scribble something corny about the "jagged cliffs" or "salty breeze" in my journal. Benedetto works in Milan for Ferrovia dello Stato and travels to Palermo every 12 days to rejoin his family for a three-day weekend before heading back to electrical maintenance at Milano Centrale.

I tell him my name and that my parents were born in Sicily and Calabria, but that I was born in Canada. I know the drill so well I can almost peel it off without an accent. I wait for the predictable reaction that a hybrid of Sicilian and Calabrian genes normally inspires in Italian-Canadians, but the irony was lost on him. Benedetto is charmed by my accent and forgives me for slipping into *Laghitano* whenever I can't quite cope with *il standard*. I notice a ring on his wedding finger and ask him if he is married. *Fidanzato*. Engagement rings for men! Who said Italians weren't liberal?

Benedetto and Silvana have been dating for nine years, but cannot afford a wedding on their paltry Sicilian salaries. Like many young men of the south, who either turn to the military or the civil service for the luxury of permanent and secure employment, after finishing school he set out to seek his fortune *la sú*.

As our train rolls to a temporary stop I hear a familiar ditty. *"Aqua minerale, café, aranciata, Coca-Cola . . ."* It can't be. *"Panini, birra, aqua, café, panini . . ."* I swear it's the same voice! Benedetto asks me what's wrong.

"It sounds like the same vendor who was here more than 10 years ago." Benedetto says it is the vendor's 18th year on the job. He's the only refreshment seller allowed. The *capo stazione* is his brother-in-law. He quickly glances into the hallway and tells me to hang onto my purse. The black market hawker and AIDS *finocchio* are coming. Just as I am about to admonish him for his paranoid, homophobic attitudes, two men enter our cabin. One is blowing a whistle while fumbling with music cassettes and the other stares blankly in front of him carrying a large knapsack. It takes seconds for them to spot my camera and disc player, and just as they are about to dive into their schtick, they recognize Benedetto and move on.

"*Disgraziati!*"

I'm speechless. He rolls his head at my naïveté. Apparently they're a team. One sells this year's San Remo hits while the other spins a story about how he got "sick." Then they use the cash they make to shoot up in the men's room. *Porcheria.* I pity Benedetto for his street savvy but 60 hours a month exposed to every archetype the peninsula has to offer would harden the greenest *terrone.*

With my Surviving Sicily tips behind me, I wish Benedetto "*Buona fortuna, belle cose,*" and disembark the train at Villa San Giovanni. As I reach the dock of the *traghetti privati*, I walk up to the ticket wicket and ask to purchase one ticket for the ferry ride to Messina. The older of the two ticket agents looks at his partner and shrugs.

The second sailor giggles, "*Si Signorina. Mille lire.*"

Bo? I hand over the money and wait for my ticket. The younger guy abandons his search for the ticket wad, blows three years of dust off a notepad, scrawls *bigletto* on a slip of paper, and slips it under the glass. I hand my *cassarecchia* ticket to the sailor directing traffic and am so captivated by the panorama that I am only mildly annoyed to be the only foot passenger bothering to pay. I head for the upper deck to admire the view.

Since my parents' separation when I was four, I have felt Sicily's proximity to the mainland mirrors my own to my father. Divorced from the continent, we still endure all the growing pains that both history and geography demand. I pray I don't run into him in Piazza del Duomo and hope to spend a quiet and restful week with my nonna.

The week *is* quiet and restful, at times. I am jostled from *parenti* to *paesani*, eat too many *arancini* and get too much sun in the company of a nice New Yorker named Pole.

Sleazy Brindisi is the hottest city on the planet. I have a clear sense of what insanity feels like as I wrestle with my pack. The sweat and smog has fused my money belt to my flesh. I fumble for the train voucher spilling the contents of my day pack onto the front deck. As I do so I feel a rough, potato-sack fabric brush up against my side.

"*Aiuto?*" the nun bending down to help collect my Europass offers with a smile.

"*Grazie.*"

She is a dead ringer for the Dominican sister who kept night watch at the nunnery in Siena. Jen and I stumbled drunkenly through the cobblestones as we heard the bells chime after lock-up hours. I skidded into the lobby just as she was rattling the keys she kept looped on the belt of her habit. Suor Gemma sternly ordered us to bed. Little did she know we were celebrating Oca's *palio* win with the neighbourhood priest!

As I examine the immaculate condition of the Suor Lucia's *au naturel* complexion I learn she has a brother in Hamilton whom she visited last summer. She was unimpressed with the CN Tower or Eaton Centre, but her nephews took her to a Jays' game when the dome was open and she ate Chinese food for the first time in her life. Her ears are invisible behind her headdress and she patiently mops her sweaty brow with her *fazzoletto* and a sigh. I ask her about wearing such dreadfully hot clothes in the sweltering and oppressive heat of Italian summers, but she simply shrugs and says it's a vocation.

That's the same response she gives me every time I venture into canonical (read Catholic) turf. I want to impress her with my education by the sisters of St. Joseph and the Basilian fathers. How does she feel about the Church's view of women in positions of responsibility? After 43 years in the community, she doesn't see any changes on the horizon given the tremendous flux that has already taken place in her tenure. Why did she become a nun?

She tells me her parents died when she was still a child. Her brothers cared for her until they moved to America. She never fancied the idea of serving a man so she decided to dedicate her life to serving God instead. Her residence cares for the elderly. She reads to them and they say the rosary together. It's not easy at times, but the convent is her home. *Buona fortuna. Vai in pace.*

For a fleeting moment, I contemplate the simple life. *Who am I kidding?* I can't live without Shoppers Drug Mart, much less flirting or bikini waxes. As I wait for the train connection to take me back to Calabria I kick myself for not taking the bus into Puglia. Frugal beginnings will me to squeeze every last cent out of my train pass. I treat myself to a coffee at a table on the *terrazza* and get caught up on my journal.

I'm recalling a moment of way too much ouzo when I see a blonde girl tear out of the café in tears. A man chases her out and pins her to the lamppost. She wails. He is twisting her arm and whispering something into her ear. I look around to make sure I am in plenty of company and stand up to ask if she is okay. I stand firm and stare him down, a skill I learned well as a child. He storms off, slapping the concrete walls as he goes by. I offer her a seat, but she prefers to sit on the curb. The waiter brings her a glass of water and calls her Silvia.

Silvia takes a sip and uses the rest to wash off her smeared mascara. It's almost time for my train. I leave her my copy of *Gente* and 10,000 lire, hoping it's enough for a taxi home. As I get up to leave she makes her way back to the curb just as her companion zooms up on his Vespa. This time he's smiling, cooing, smoothing her hair. I can't make out what he's saying, but I know in the long run she's in for it as she climbs onto the backseat and they zoom away.

Riding the rails at night is creepy. I ditch my reserved seat after an exhibitionist positions himself so that I can witness his pleasure through the glass reflection. I opt for a seat near a mother travelling with her three children. When they depart I am left alone at my final station. There are three or four people standing on the platform as I head into the *capo stazione's* office. I muster up all the charm I can, given my unruly appearance, saunter up to the counter, and in my very best *italiano* sweetly inquire if there is anywhere I can find a public phone at this hour. There are times when it helps being a woman travelling alone, and in a country where local calls are not free, at any time of the evening, the station master is happy to oblige. I assure him it is inter-provincial and will only take a second as I ring my Zio Gigino to tell him that I will be in Amantea via Castiglione in 25 minutes. *"Scusi,* but you should avoid Castiglione at this hour. It's better to wait here and take the direct train to Amantea in 45 minutes."

I opt for the later train and impress the station master and his assistant with tales of my telephone job interview in Barcelona and the teaching post that is waiting for me back home. They fill me in on the *concorsi nazionali* that are necessary for teaching or any government job in Europe.

I am the only person on the direct train to Amantea. Francesco, the ticketing guy, is not convinced that my legs could be *that* smooth or olive-toned and has to caress them *just one more time* to make sure. I am about to tell him to piss off when an older married couple takes the seats opposite me. Francesco wanders off and I thank them for their interference. As the train pulls into Amantea I can see Zio Gigino's warm smile and open arms waving from the platform.

"How was your trip?" he asks as he dumps my ruck-sack in the living room. The smell of flour and oregano has lingered from the fresh focaccia Zia prepared this morning. I fill my aunt, uncle, and cousins in on my travels, omitting the saucier parts, and Zia marvels at how *gli Americani* take risks Italians would never dream of.

"San Francesco di Paola, protect her," Zia prays, making the sign of the cross. *"Domani a messa!"* she orders as she clears the table and sends me off to bed. I fall into the most miraculous sleep I have had since I left home and rise early for Sunday morning mass. Reflecting on my Eurail odyssey, I think of San Francesco and figure I owe him a couple of *Padre Nostros*.

The View from Here

GISELLE SIGNORONI

Thirty degrees in the shade, no clouds in sight. Not 24 hours earlier I had gotten off my flight from Toronto to join my husband in the quaint town of Griante on Lake Como, one of those Italian villages that seem to change little with the passing of the decades, giving you the false belief that you know the place.

This is where my parents were born, fell in love, and then left only to return year after year. For more than four decades this village, worthy of first kisses and last rites, has been my second home. My brother and I buried both our parents here. How will this sojourn change me? It used to be that nothing changed. Now it seems nothing stays the same. I have learned that this place changes me more than I change it.

Today's trail will take me up 1,400 metres and I will trace with Antonio, my Italian-born husband, the steps that we took after our wedding in Griante over 20 years ago. Today, like that May day in 1981, it is just the two of us on the way up. I can feel my body letting go, taken over by the smells and the air and the earth. The seasons here reflect a good life with spring long and mellow, summer intense and flavourful, fall bountiful and surprising, and winter chill but sweet. Although the path is in the pre-Alps, today it feels like a tropical jungle. The heat and the bugs are intense. I dream of being here in another season.

The sudden rustling of leaves and branches behind me makes me turn abruptly and cry out.

She is smaller than me and completely black, a figure covered in a large, sheer black veil. I feel shame for showing surprise and fear at the sight of this beautiful woman, skin the colour of midnight and eyes that seem moonlit.

Apologetically she utters, "I am so sorry. . . . I didn't mean to scare you."

I pretend to have simply been momentarily startled and allow her to pass. She is leaner and faster and joins my husband up ahead where the trail is growing denser and harder to follow. They take a short cut up a steep incline, but when I catch up to them, the three of us find the path again and continue to hike at our own pace. When we reach the peak, the woman and I chat in English. I learn that she is visiting from England and hiking the four valleys from Como to the north end of the lake alone. She is dressed in long sleeves and long pants and covers herself with the black veil because of the bugs and the overgrown branches. She calls a friend in Florence each evening. She can't chat for long because she needs to reach her next destination before dark. Antonio and I watch in admiration as she picks up her small knapsack and moves on.

When I tell my Italian family and friends down in the village of the encounter they are convinced she is *spostata*, insane. Perhaps she has escaped from some local institution. Perhaps I should report her to the authorities. Might innocent people be at risk? They are not completely serious, but they are not joking either.

I am not suspicious; I am respectful and grateful, grateful to Mariarosa Venini and Gino Ortelli, my parents, whose immigration to Canada has given me the ability to look beyond race, religion, gender, and class. My parents came to Canada for an adventure rather than survival. Were they were drawn *to* something or *from* something? They *chose* to leave Italy, a fact that made it harder to get through times of loneliness, but their choice has made them proud of their children's achievements: good education, good jobs, good partners.

My parents made a decision that set me apart. How could I be Italian-Canadian and have no *zii* or *zie*, *nonni* or *nonne*, *cugini* or *cugine* with whom to spend *Natale* and *Pasqua*? I longed to fit the stereotype, to have an identity, to have parents who had a mortgage rather than a lease, who drank wine and not whiskey, who canned tomatoes and made biscotti, who held big celebrations with families and friends. Our gatherings were small and quiet in Canada as well as in Italy.

I was the only Italian-Canadian in my school of many Italian-Canadians who grew up in an apartment rather than a house. I grew up in Toronto after arriving there in 1962 from Montreal, where I was born. My Italian-Canadian friends were not allowed to visit because their parents imagined I lived in small, inadequate, and unsafe quarters. I felt an affinity to Roberto Benigni who, upon receiving his Oscar, thanked his parents for having been born poor, but not poor in spirit. I was grateful to have experienced 2050 Keele Street with all its nationalities, religions, colours, and smells. I thank Mrs. Mistry from India, Eleonora from Greece, Sara from Calabria, the families from Australia, Argentina, Jamaica, New Zealand, and others for introducing my mother, the homemaker and local babysitter, to the world.

Our balcony on the sixth floor faced west toward the airport. It offered too many sunsets to remember while the hallways and elevators offered the aromas of world cuisines. The place did not feel like the cage my Italian home-owning friends imagined it to be and I learned to not be embarrassed by what friends perceived as the stench of the foreign. This modest space was my home. The small outdoor pool and tennis court were my summer camp. Italian-Canadian friends would retreat to their cool basements and backyard gardens and I to what was to become my favourite element, water.

As a teenager I was given more freedom to travel than any of my peers thanks to the free passes my father got from working at Canadian Pacific. Kids thought he was a pilot, but he was a simple travel agent whose job gave me the gift of the world. I had gone from feeling upset that I didn't fit the stereotype to thanking God that I was "different."

The meaning of my past is forever changing. The definition of my village, my family, my life now, is relative to what it once was and will be. Both homes, like lovers, give me a sense of, a view of, myself. The caresses and compliments, like breezes and showers, warm and cool me. My understanding depends on how much I allow myself to enjoy my surroundings. Canada, with its expanses and reputation for humanity, Griante, with its beauty and sensuality, caress me simultaneously, both of them familiar and exotic.

With each visit to Griante I learn to embrace change and am reminded that I shall never know all there is to be known about any place, any culture, any past. Like lovers, our knowledge of each other will always be incomplete. The stories we tell each other become small mirrors held up to each other, each reflecting new truths, realities, sacred dimensions, one small piece at a time . . . *poco poco*. Depending on the light and the looker, the teller and the tale, the story reflected will change.

For almost half a century I have lived in two places at the same time. My heart and mind belong to both. In a few days I will be returning once again with Adriana, my 11-year-old daughter, to Griante. She is already imagining the smells and tastes of the place and the birds and children that pause during the hot summer afternoon. I can tell that she is expecting everything to be just as she left it last year. The relatives are ageless in her eyes and she cannot imagine the place without them.

But I see the chill of winter even though it is 30 degrees in the shade, and so, each visit, each piece of bread broken together with the young and not so young, each hike in the mountains surrounding Griante, each swim in my beloved Lake Como, is a gift. When I am gone I will be heartened if both Adriana and my older son, Roberto, will be able to say as I can say, "I loved two unique worlds and learned from both, but their greatest gift was the ability to see 'the other' in myself."

Down Three Steps

MIRELLA (SICHIROLLO) PATZER

A single bird trilled high in the olive branches as the early morning Italian summer sun caressed the back of my neck and shoulders; a day fully in bloom. I sat on the edge of the fountain in the piazza of the village where my mother was born: here she played as a child, survived the devastation of war, and married. I looked around at the town that held so many memories for her while I waited for the bus to the seaside town of Ortona.

I stood where my mamma must have stood many years before when she left her home to immigrate. Her presence was everywhere, floating on the breeze that swept my hair, on the warm cobblestones, in the very air I breathed. She was the fourth daughter of a family of vintners that had enjoyed an uncomplicated life here for generations until the war came. Their home was the first to be bombed. The family fled to the sanctuary of a nearby cave where they survived eight cold, rainy months drinking river water and scavenging root vegetables. Afterward, they spent years rebuilding what the war ruined. This was my mother's childhood, unlike my Canadian one where the smells from my mother's kitchen greeted me after school and I slept safely tucked in my small bed at night.

As I looked about, the only evidence of war was a crumbling shell of a home at the far end of the street and a small plaque in the piazza bearing the names of some of the dead. Newer homes now stood in place of those destroyed. People bustled about conducting their daily business. It was obvious no one wanted to remember what had happened there so long ago.

My roots were in the rich soil of this land that had

been in my family for generations and was as old as the grapevines and fruit trees that grew upon it. I came to seek my future within my past, to understand a way of life denied to me when fate lured my parents to Canada, and to savour a culture untarnished by the adjustments of immigration. Today, I had a mission. I was 18 years old and the spontaneity of this first romantic adventure enchanted me. In youthful naïveté, I fully expected to discover answers by the time I returned home. Little did I know I was to discover much more.

~

Several months before, in the kitchen of our modest Calgary home, my mother and I had shared a cup of tea and a sorry tale long buried. She talked of the small village not far from the Adriatic coast where she had been born and how as a child she endured the horrors of the war. Several years after the war ended, she fell in love with my father who had journeyed from northern Italy in search of work. He found it on my grandfather's lands, harvesting the abundant grapes hanging plump and ripe from the family vines. It was 1954, and by the next year's grape harvest their first child would be born.

But in her eighth month of pregnancy, a strange illness fell upon my mother. Asiatic influenza, part of a pandemic, spread across Europe. For days she suffered, and in her delirium, she dreamed.

Maria, her mamma's best friend and long-time neighbour, came to her in a dream and hovered over her bed.

"Ella, I came to ask for your help, for a *piacere*; a favour. I need to borrow money from you, Ella."

"Maria, I have no money. We have been married for only a year. Our lives together have only just begun and every lira must be saved to make a good life for our baby."

"If you do not have money, then go to my husband and ask him for it. He is a good man and he will lend it to you. If he is not home, then go into our house and stored in the top drawer of the dresser in our bedroom, under the bed linens, you will find some money. Go and get it for me. I must purchase a small plot of land down three steps and to the right."

Soon after, Mamma's fever broke and she began to feel better. A week later she gave birth to a son. She and my father were happy and they named the baby Antonio. But he would not nurse. Fearing her milk was tainted, her friend Giovanna, who had recently given birth herself, tried to nurse Antonio, but with the same result. A doctor was called, but he only shook his head and whispered that Antonio had been born with the influenza. There was nothing to be done but to wait and pray. Mamma's eyes welled with tears.

Antonio died in her arms four days later.

"I barely remember the funeral other than it was a cold, rainy day in January. I had never seen such a small white coffin. Your father carried it to the church by himself. He refused to allow anyone to help. The entire village followed behind us. After the service, we placed Antonio in a hearse and we travelled to Ortona to bury him. When we arrived at the cemetery, our solemn procession passed by the lonely graves until we found the one meant for Antonio. I screamed when I saw where it lay and fell to my knees at the sight of it — down three steps and to the right — just as Maria had foretold."

～

Several people had gathered now near the fountain where I waited to board the bus. I stood and followed, smiling at the driver as I carefully slid my lira into the coin collector. I chose a window seat near the middle of the bus, grateful for the morning breeze. As the bus pulled away, I came to understand why my mother left. Too much sorrow existed here; a new life held promises that the old one could not deliver.

"You look like your mother," a voice said.

I turned and my eyes met hers as she moved from her seat across the aisle to sit beside me.

"How do you know me? How do you know my mother?" I asked, puzzled. I studied her. She had a pleasant face already tanned by the sun.

"San Leonardo is a small village and news travels fast. I heard you were here and I am glad to meet you. I was a friend of your mother. My name is Giovanna."

She asked about my mother and our lives in Canada. As she spoke, a new vision of my mamma came to life, one full of the vitality and joy of youth, of the pranks and mischief of the young, and of the carefree passion of a young Italian girl who had once lived there.

I learned Giovanna never left San Leonardo. Instead, she married, had three children, and still farmed the same vineyards her family owned for generations. She worked mornings at a local shoe store for extra spending money. My mother might have enjoyed this same life and I could have too. I lamented the loss. Like all conversations with strangers, however, we soon ran out of things to say.

Giovanna broke the silence first. "Where are you going?"

"I promised my mother I would visit my brother's grave, but I'm not exactly sure where the cemetery is, and of course, I will need to purchase some flowers first."

"Ah yes," she said in a solemn voice. "I remember the sadness of it. I tried to nurse the baby, but he could not."

"She has never forgotten your kindness during that terrible time."

"There is nothing I would not have done for your mother. She was my friend. I have missed her all these years. I am on my way to work not very far from the cemetery. I am a little early this morning and could accompany you there, if you wish."

I was glad for the offer.

As the bus wound its way down the narrow highway and around the sharp curves that led to Ortona, an unusual melancholy set in. My mamma's past had become my present and it hovered in the air like the scent of the grapes that decorated the countryside.

Soon the verdant slopes of the olive-clustered landscape gave way to more houses and with it came the first scents of sea breeze that graced the port town of Ortona. As the bus made its way through the quaint streets in the centre of town, Giovanna pointed out the landmarks — the town's central fountain, the walkway over the port, the Church of San Tommaso. Giovanna gathered her purse as the bus came to a halt in the centre square.

Together we walked up a steep hill to the tall iron

gates of the cemetery's marble walls. Just in front of the gates was a kindly woman selling white carnations and daisies. Giovanna waited while I purchased a bouquet then guided me through the sombre rows, past the family mausoleums, beyond the walls that housed neatly tended tombstones until we finally arrived in the small area for children. We traced each row, reading each tombstone, but we could not find Antonio.

We walked to the office and asked a nearby grave-digger who was already busy at his work. At Giovanna's inquiry, he leaned against his shovel to wipe the sweat from his brow. Then he pointed in the direction of the children's graves and offered to help us. Still we could not find him.

"Graves are often exhumed after 20 years and the bones placed in a smaller box then sealed away in the wall of the mausoleum somewhere. *Mi dispiace, signorina.*" And with that, the gravedigger left us.

Giovanna looked at her watch; she had to leave or risk being late. She took my hand in both of hers and apologized for not having found my brother. Then, kissing me on both cheeks, she wished me well and sent her best wishes to my mother.

As Giovanna turned to leave, I gripped her arm. "No wait. Please wait." Behind me was a row of large overgrown bushes. In the middle of the row of graves where we stood were odd, flat stones, untended.

Before me were three steps — down and to the right. There, I met my brother for the first time.

Giovanna paled and made the sign of the cross.

I felt his presence as sure as the gentle breeze and the sun that warmed the air. An older brother who would have watched over me as I grew, who would have blessed our lives in ways I could not fathom was no longer unknown to me.

Unashamed of my tears, I stared at the tiny picture of the small baby on the marble tombstone who had known my mother as I did now, as if for the first time.

The Vigil

CARLA MARIA LUCCHETTA

I wear my dead around my neck.
  This single pearl on a thin, gold chain, knotted near the clasp, belonged to my sister Donna. I can't even remember how I came to possess it. Today I place it around my neck, beside the silver Mary, to conjure my long-dead sister.

The day my sister Donna died, a single red rose bloomed from the parched bush in our garden. I noticed it while I waited on the veranda for Mom to come home from the hospital. Donna and I bookend the family with 11 years and three siblings between us. She skipped two grades and was already in high school by the time I came along. I barely knew her, and then she was gone.

That was June 18, 1975. I had just finished Grade 9, but my summer fun was delayed that day by the chore of washing the kitchen floor. Mom insisted on doing it the old-fashioned way — on hands and knees, scrub, wax, and then buff, using the heavy machine that danced me around the kitchen. Halfway through the job I got distracted by the mouth-watering aroma of Nonna's *tagliani* soup drifting up from her basement kitchen.

Then the phone rang. My brother-in-law's slightly frantic voice on the other end asked, "Is your mom home?"

"She's at work. Is something wrong?"

"If she comes home, tell her to phone the hospital right away."

Why wouldn't he just try her at the office? I went back to my task, only to be interrupted a few minutes later by Paul's mother.

"Hello dear. Is your mother home?"

"No, she's not. Is anything wrong? Paul just called too."

"Do you know where she is?"

"I think she's at work. Did something happen to Donna?"

"Just have your mom call the hospital if she comes home."

"Okay, but I don't think she's coming home soon." It was mid-afternoon.

I hung up the phone, but stayed close to it. I wished someone other than Nonna was home. She barely spoke English and I barely spoke Italian. Usually we managed to communicate in a broken version of either language. I went back to my scrubbing.

A little while later my two aunts walked into the house. "Is your father home?" Auntie Mary asked.

"No." Why were they there in the middle of the day? They usually traipsed past our living room and down the stairs to visit my grandparents on weekends. "I'm the only one here, except for Nonna."

"Let's go to your room," Auntie Ange said. I followed them to my bedroom, the one I used to share with all three of my sisters. The one where I often lay awake worrying that my sick sister would die.

"Donna is dead," Auntie Ange told me, her face stone.

"It happened earlier today. And, if you need to cry, do it now, because your mother is going to need you to be strong."

~

She'd been sick for two years. One Sunday we came home from church to find her waiting for us on our porch. She had been out west with Paul on a delayed honeymoon, and they weren't due back for another few days. It was clear that something was wrong. Her stomach was so bloated she looked eight months pregnant.

Mom rushed out of the car. "What's wrong? Why are you home? Are you alone?"

Donna explained that she'd become ill in Vancouver and Paul had put her on a plane. They couldn't both afford to fly so he was hitchhiking back. She was admitted to the hospital and diagnosed with blood clots, treated with medication, and discharged within a matter of days. Paul took her back to the hospital a week later when her symptoms recurred. This time we knew she was really sick.

Mom came home from the hospital, gathered us together and said, "God needs Donna more than we do." I waited for her to say something more, but that was it.

"What does she mean?" I later asked Frances.

"She means Donna's gonna die."

~

But she didn't die. Not then. Over the next year, Donna went back and forth to the hospital for operations and extended stays. She had four in total, but there were times when she was home and everyone tried to get back to normal. Donna even went back to her job at the group home down the street from us.

Mom and Dad fought a lot, but now it was always about Donna and tests and operations, things I didn't want to hear, even by accident. "Don't worry," they kept saying whenever I got up enough courage to ask a question. But how could I not? Mom was exhausted from work and from looking after Donna. She'd hardly had any time to recover from worrying about Maryanne, the second oldest, who'd just had a baby and gotten married, in that order, at only 19. Mom had a short temper and a permanently furrowed brow.

All I wanted was to get out of the house and hang out at Denise's but Mom thought I was over there too much. Sulking in my bedroom was as close as I got to escape. I'd stomp off and slam my door, a ploy to get Mom to come after me. One time it was Donna who opened my door. She sat down on the edge of my bed, crouching to avoid hitting her head on the top bunk.

"What's wrong?" she asked.

"Nothing," I lied. I hadn't spent much time with her since she'd gotten married three years earlier, and certainly not since she'd been sick — Mom and Dad didn't want me to worry. I was still getting used to the new way she looked. Her eyes were twice the size they used to be and I was afraid to look into them.

"Don't be too hard on Mom, Carla. She has a lot to deal with."

"*She's* never home," I said, "so why should she care if *I* am or not?"

"She cares, and so do I. You can always come to me. Okay?"

"Okay." It didn't take long for her to win me over. She had always been my favourite babysitter, the only one who didn't flinch when I shouted, "You're not my boss!"

～

At the hospital a few months earlier, I had been afraid of Donna in her sick bed. Gone was her long, beautiful, thick hair. Her tall, lanky frame looked lost in the stiff folds of hospital sheets. The tubes and wires sticking in and out of her were too frightening to even be a curiosity to me. I didn't understand her illness except that it had something to do with her liver and blood clots and some kind of tube that would help the blood flow. I picked most of this up from conversations I overheard when I was supposed to be sleeping. No one spoke to me about Donna and I didn't talk about it beyond the walls of our house unless to relatives who only shook their heads and looked mad.

That day I stood in the shadows at the back of the hospital room trying not to look.

When we were leaving Mom said, "Aren't you going to kiss your sister goodbye?"

Tentatively, I walked to the bed. What if what she had was catching? I leaned over and tried to kiss her without actually touching her.

"I think she's going to die," Mom said on the way to the car. That was the last time I saw her.

~

The night she died I desperately needed my mother. I wanted to disappear into her arms, though I was too old for that now. But, remembering the words of my aunt I tried not to show my need, or my fear. Time was standing still and moving so fast all at the same time. Even with the endless parade of aunts, uncles, and cousins hugging and crying our house was silent. So many things were wrong. Donna was the first grandchild, the pride of the family. Donna and Paul were practically newlyweds when she got sick. They'd been childhood sweethearts since the age of 13. My sister had become the glue that held my parents' fragile marriage together.

"Goddamn doctors," my father's rant broke the quiet. "I'm gonna sue the shit outta them." Mom, Dad, and Paul had to decide about an autopsy, which didn't make any sense to me.

"But, I thought she died because of her liver," I said.

Mom waved me away, "Go sit with your sister."

I was trying not to be mad at Frances for being the one Dad hugged, instead of me, even though I was the one with him when he heard the news. I settled in beside Maryanne instead who sat absently rocking her baby. "I guess I'm the oldest now," she said.

"Where's your brother?" Mom said, breaking out of a hushed conversation to do a head count.

I pointed to the corner where my brother had folded himself, trying to look invisible. All present and accounted for, but somehow, for the very first time in my life, I felt entirely alone.

~

The only thing I really remember from the day of the viewing was eating Chinese food for the first time. In between the morning and afternoon visitation times everyone except Mom went across to the Chinese restaurant. I felt strange without her close by, but I nevertheless doused my chicken balls and rice in gobs of sweet-and-sour sauce, and read my fortune: "You will find great love." I thought about Mike, the boy next door and the subject of my torturous crush, and I wondered if he'd heard what had happened and would be at the funeral.

At the funeral parlour I slipped my hand into my mother's. She held it tightly, squashing her Kleenex into my palm. I ventured a sideways peek at her tired, older face. If Mom fell apart, then what would happen to us? I didn't even know where my father was. Since Donna's death, he barely came near us. I put my other hand over hers and squeezed to say, "I'm still here."

I had attended other funerals before this one. Mom never made us look at the dead body if we didn't want to and afterwards we always did something fun. When Nonno Longo died, we went to Christmas Fairyland.

This time I stood right beside the closed casket as people came and went, kissing and hugging my mom and me. When I spotted my friend Denise and her mom I ran to see them.

"It's okay to cry," Denise's mom said, pressing a Kleenex into my hand. But I didn't feel like it then. Why was it okay for me to cry in a public, but not alone with my Mom at home?

The funeral was early in the morning the next day. The last time I had walked up the aisle at St. Andrew's it was for Donna and Paul's wedding in February, less than three years earlier. I'd seen Mom and Dad kiss that day. I had worn a blue floral bib dress with a built-in white blouse and a big ruffle on the bottom.

This time I walked up the aisle behind Donna's dead body in my new Jesus boots, and I had to keep stopping to hike up the knee-high criss-cross straps. The mass was longer than a regular Sunday one, but Mom didn't even try to stop me fidgeting. I kept imagining Donna opening up the casket and proclaiming, "I'm alive!" Why couldn't that happen? Why couldn't we go back a few days to when she was just sick, not dead? Why couldn't Mom talk to us and Dad be less angry? It seemed appropriate to ask these questions in the House of the Lord. I looked over at Mom on her knees, her head bowed, hands clasped together, her lips moving in prayer, and I wondered how she could still have so much faith.

~

Three months after Donna's death Mom and Dad had a fight, at first not louder than the others. In fact, not loud at all. Dad stormed out of the house, practically pulling the door off its hinges and slamming it hard. Mom shouted after him, "If you walk out now, you're not coming back." It had been a long time since Mom had raised her voice. I waited for him to come back, for the post-fight fallout, more doors slamming, hurling insults, a plate thrown across the room. After a couple of hours, and only because Mom insisted, I reluctantly moved my vigil to my bedroom where I tried to sleep and to stay alert at the same time.

I woke in the morning to the news that Dad had slept in the car in our driveway all night, and Mom wouldn't let him back in. I couldn't even pretend to be unhappy about this. All my life I'd been hearing from one of my parents, "When Carla's 16, I'm leaving." Well, here I was only 14 and they were finally making good on their word. I began Grade 10 that September feeling lighter. During summer vacation my sister had died and my parents had separated, but all I could feel was relief.

~

The single red rose that bloomed on the day my sister died wilted the next day. I don't think I ever told anyone that.

Talking Pictures

FRANCESCA SCHEMBRI

On December 27, 1994 Carm looked at her daughter Santina's framed photograph and whispered, "How can she still smile?"

"She smiles because she's happy, finally," I answered. But, Carm wasn't talking to me; she was talking to herself.

Holding both her daughter's and her late husband's

pictures, she continued, "I wish you were here by my side, caressing my hair, waiting for me."

I rose and left her to her thoughts, but I stood outside the door for a few minutes and listened. "For 25 long years, lying on these white sheets, I have tried to visualize the two of us side-by-side in bed. My nights have been lonely and my bed too large, my life too empty and my heart as dry as my tearless eyes."

For a few seconds it was quiet, then the shuffle of footsteps, followed by the squeaky sound of the old mattress' springs disrupted the silence.

She whispered again, more quietly, as if her lips barely moved, "I remember the rocking chair in which you spent countless nights rocking our baby to sleep, while I was busy with the chores. Santina's birth was the loneliest event of my life. I resented you for dying! A widow with a baby! It was so unfair having one with out the other! Santina's birth, unlike Vincenzo's, did not bring me joy, or any cause for celebration. I did not want her to be born fatherless. The almond cookies, the pink *confetti* and the *amaretto* were not shared with our friends. No one was invited to meet the baby; no one invited for her baptism, as no one had been invited to our son's wedding, years later. These weren't celebrations.

"Vincenzo's wedding ceremony rekindled memories

of our own wedding day. Ours was shortly after the war and my mother could not afford to buy me a wedding gown, so I wore my older sister's. I remember you whispering to me, ' You look like an angel in this simple dress, my Carmelina,' while picking a fresh orange blossom from my headpiece. 'I will always keep it close to my heart, as my *porta fortuna*.' We kissed, do you remember?

"The trip to Canada two months later was our honeymoon. The *Urania Seconda* was an old ship you suspected had been used in the war. Yet, I thought it better than Cinderella's carriage. More than two weeks and I was seasick for most of it. To make matters worse, we had to sleep in separate quarters. To get some privacy, we used to sneak out at night. One of those nights, while the watchful sea serenaded us, our son was conceived. My first born, a Canadian.

"We knew that to make it, to *fare l'America*, would not be easy. I will never forget that December evening, in 1954, when we took a stroll downtown to admire Toronto's Christmas decorations. The department store windows were filled with such colourful merchandise. You got caught up in the moment and spent what little money you had on a carillon, a music box, for me. How happy I was every time I listened to 'Silent Night' and thought that in our hearts, we were filthy rich, *amore*. In spite of all the money struggles, we were happy.

"Everything went as planned, until your accident. The doorbell rang while I was cooking supper. Vincenzo went to open it, thinking it was his friend from school. He hollered from the living room — a police officer was asking for me. The newspapers reported your death as just another accident in the construction industry, '*Un Italiano Sepolto Vivo*' reported the *Corriere Canadese*, and the *Toronto Daily Star* said that Italian immigrants in the construction industry were frequently being buried alive. For most, it was a predictable casualty, even welcome, just one less immigrant living in Toronto.

"Safety regulations had not been established. A bag of cement had covered your whole body. You died such a cruel death, and I was not there to comfort you. You should have died in my arms; I should have been there to close your eyes with my lips.

"The house was filled with relatives, friends, and *paesani* uttering, 'Poor woman ... pregnant, she shouldn't ... Who is going to take care of her after burying him?' Only happily married women should carry babies in their wombs, not phantoms like me. I called your name, over and over."

Santina was born five months after, but Carm did not

celebrate. Santina's birthdays were not celebrated until she was 14. Vincenzo took her to MacDonald's and to the movie that year. Carmelina said they did not have money to spend on frivolous things, but even when Santina worked part time, she was not allowed to invite her friends over for a party.

Shortly after her husband's death, Carmelina began to babysit the children of relatives and neighbours in her home. During this time Carmelina dressed in black and did not go anywhere other than to the church to attend Sunday mass. Vicenzo, at 12, worked part-time jobs, while going to school.

As if responding to my thoughts, Carmelina resumed her whispering. "Vincenzo was the only man in our household. He was proud of bringing money to his family. After high school he moved to Montreal to earn a Law Degree in a French University.

"You should have seen him — how handsome he looked in his robe. He bore such a striking resemblance to you, my love. I was very proud of him. But, having an ethnic name, at least in those days, was a liability, so he changed his name and married the daughter of a prominent French-Canadian lawyer. That was 1979. Your son was not Vincenzo Di Martino, but Vince St. Martin! Forgive him, *gioia mia*.

"Santina did not make me so proud. She was 17 when she started going out with her *mangiacake* friend. I objected to it because I wanted to protect her reputation. I did not want our relatives saying that because she did not have a father, her mother hadn't raised her properly. I told her to get engaged first, then she could go out with him. She said that this was the Italian way but not his. He was young and wasn't thinking of marriage. So, though I did not approve it, she moved out. From that day forward, I decided not to see or speak to her again."

Carm's first months after Santina moved out were filled with resentment and anger. I did not take Santina's side, but I also did not help the situation. As I did when Santina was only six years old and her mother slapped her, I did not interfere, and Santina felt abandoned. She had been invited to attend one of her classmates' birthday parties, but Carm was very angry and bitter and did not allow it. "How dare you ask to go to a party while we're still mourning your father!" she yelled. Santina, lonely, disappointed and neglected, retaliated by insulting her mother and calling her a D.P. and a "stupid immigrant." She was punished. Santina resented my silence and did not forgive me for not supporting her.

"*Carmelina, vieni in cucina con me,*" I said now, re-entering the bedroom.

She looked at me and asked, "Where did I make a mistake?"

"You didn't, you did what you could," I tried in vain to reassure her but she ignored me and spoke again to her husband, picking up where she left off. "Santina moved out. She was angry I did not approve of her decision. In my mind, she was a *buttana*. She had dishonoured our name and I couldn't forgive her for it. Do you know what she said to me? 'You don't even know I exist! You are living in the past! Wake up!' Pride blinded me. I turned my back on her. If I were to accept her, I would lose face, and worse, I would lose the support of our relatives.

"I was very sick, deep in depression, they said, and stayed in the hospital for several days. Vincenzo brought her to visit me. I did not recognize her at first. She had dyed her hair blond, in an attempt to look less Italian. She was very pale, like she had no blood left in her veins. Her pupils were so dilated that she looked like a mad person. Why was she looking so sick? 'What did that son of a bitch do to you? Why don't you come home to your mother? Don't you have a family?' I asked, but her lips were pinched, like a slice of the moon.

"Vincenzo said, 'You need to be very understanding with her, she's not well. Drugs have made her sick.' I knew better: the evil eye had been cast against her, the *maìa* had made her *spiritata*, crazy, not the drugs. Vincenzo said it would take time, a lot of will power and all the support and love she could get to recover.

"What did I know about drugs? *Caro mio*, our beautiful daughter was a scary sight. It broke my heart to see her this way. At the rehabilitation centre they called her Sandy instead of Santina. The place was run by Italian nuns and a priest. I talked endlessly to him about my troubles. With God's help, she returned home, got a part-time job and went back to school. She took most of the courses at night and worked during the day.

"Yet, I was afraid I would lose her again. I spent many sleepless nights sitting on the floor outside her bedroom and feeling helpless. My responsibility to her was not stronger than my responsibility to my culture though. I should have been there for her, as any mother would have been, I let her down one more time. One night, she suddenly screamed at me, 'What the hell are you doing? What do you want? What the hell do you want?' I retaliated with, 'Don't you understand? It's late; I can't do a damn thing any more, *capisci*. Go to bed, go!'

"Santina moved out again, this time permanently. A few months later the paramedics found her in her bedroom; she had suffered an overdose. When they arrived, she was as cold as ice. We buried her next to your grave. Have you seen her yet? Is she as beautiful as she looks in this picture?

"For so many years I have been an immigrant in Toronto and I still do not know where I belong. I have survived by writing a new page of our romance every night. Yet, motherhood has overwhelmed me. Was I not suited for it? Was I afraid of it? Or was I simply afraid of changing my way of thinking and my lifestyle? I was a widow and a stubborn, lonely woman. I could have taken Santina's advice and learned English, worked outside the house, opened up a store, interacted with people other than Italians, become more Canadian, but something stopped me. Since you left, the winds of time have brought many changes: people have walked on the moon, countries have gone to war and made peace, others have changed their names, but I remained the same. I live in the past, frightened by my own limitations and desires, my loneliness."

Carm murmured these last words before drifting off to sleep: "I would like to find you at the last station, to be held in your arms again. I am getting tired now, and I need you more than ever. Your spirit comforts me. Will you be able to recognize me? I have changed so!"

I went to the kitchen to make tea, thinking that a trip

to the old country would do her good. As I re-entered her room, I stepped into a pool of blood dripping from an open cut on her wrist.

This time the paramedics were called to help her, and they fought to keep her alive as they had her daughter. In the emergency room a team of doctors and nurses worked rapidly. It wasn't easy for them to bring Carmelina's body to life again, but they did, though her soul never quite recovered.

In Living Colour

ROSANNA BATTIGELLI

I am staring death in the eye at the dawning of the millennium.

"He is having a heart attack right now," the doctor says. Is having, not had. Now. Still.

"Right now?" I repeat, squeezing the patient's hand. My father. I listen to the doctor's explanations of test results. "Can I get a priest?" My Catholic upbringing tells me this *must* be done.

A few minutes later, a priest arrives, murmurs the appropriate prayers for the family, and leaves. We take turns in the emergency room, each uttering words of encouragement, words of love. I bide my time in the congested waiting area.

I breathe rhythmically to stay relaxed. If his fate is death, then my father will be at peace, having suffered declining health the past several years due to the insidious progression of Parkinson's. If it is life, then we will face the challenges as they come.

"The reality is, your father has a 10 per cent chance of pulling through . . ." the specialist says a few hours later, on the first day of the year 2000. The Y2K anxiety of the last few weeks has gone, only to be replaced by another.

But my father beats the odds. He's still alive a week later. He begins to show more signs of life; he pulls off his intravenous tubes. I take the lunch shift so my mother can go home and rest. I encourage him with words he probably used on me. "Open wide now. You need to eat so you can get strong. Peas are good for you. . . ." He can't feed himself, he can't walk, and he can't talk. I listen to myself having a one-way conversation, talking about anything, everything.

"Hey, Dad, you know what I saw in my backyard yesterday? A partridge, and not a little one either. Remember all the ones you used to bring home when you went out hunting with Joe? I never really liked the taste when I was young. Mom always made it with tomato sauce; she made everything you brought home with tomato sauce: wild mushrooms, rabbits, ducks.

"You *did* make a better life for us here, Dad. Oh, I know times were lean when we were young. Mom sewed all our clothes, even our coats, to save money. I imagine Christmas must have been hard on both of you, especially those first few years after we emigrated, and with four young children to feed and clothe. Thank goodness you were able to make a garden in the backyard, just like in the old country. All those peas, zucchini, beans, and tomatoes! We never lacked for vegetables, that's for sure. And I know we did our share of complaining about them, especially dandelion greens! They were so bitter! And how embarrassing to bring an Anglophone friend home to the smell!"

My father doesn't respond. The slightest inclination of his head is the only indication I have that he may have understood. Perhaps he will never regain his speech.

He proves me wrong. His voice is raspy, incomprehensible at times, but the words begin to come. As the days pass, my conversations are no longer completely one-sided. My father tells me about the pigeons he saw. He asks me if I want a peach or a pear. He enquires as to the sausages hanging as they cure. He talks about his father as if he were still alive. He believes he is in the old country. He waves to a friend who isn't there.

He has been diagnosed with glaucoma. I ask him if he likes my new jacket. He says he does. I ask him what colour it is. He says black. My jacket is red.

Sorrowfully, I think about the colour being leached from his life, fading like a photograph exposed to too much sunlight.

Memories return like snapshots: my father comforting me after a bad dream; helping me with Grade 5 math; buying me a huge blackboard for my 11th birthday; puttering in his garden; raising rabbits and chickens; laughing at the antics of my baby daughter; holding my newborn son 13 years ago; learning he has Parkinson's disease; becoming stiffer as his illness progresses; crying when I rub his aching back with liniment; doing "Tai Chi for Parkinson's" video exercises; squeezing my hand in the emergency room. . . .

Visiting hours are over. I kiss him gently, murmuring, "I love you" directly in his ear. I wait. He squeezes my hand more tightly than usual.

Without opening his eyes, he utters a muffled reply, "I love you, too."

Tearfully, I pray that my father is blessed with sweet dreams. In brilliant colour.

Acknowledgements

The 18 women of this collective wish to thank our editor, Joy Gugeler, and ECW Press. Joy has worked overtime, and under pressure, to edit our stories so they can be powerful and true. She's been supportive, encouraging, and respectful. The journey from story idea to published book has been a roller coaster ride and we thank Joy for sharing the thrills and chills of the ride with us. *Mamma Mia!*

Recommended Reading

GENERAL

Bagnell, Kenneth. *Canadese: A Portrait of The Italian Canadians*. Toronto: Macmillan of Canada, 1989.

Barolini, Helen. *Aldus and His Dream Book: An Illustrated Essay*. New York: Italica Press, 1992.

Charon, Milly, ed. *Between Two Worlds: The Canadian Immigrant Experience*. Montreal: Nuage Editions, 1988.

Coletta McLean, Maria. *My Father Came from Italy*. Vancouver: Raincoast, 2000.

Di Giovanni, Morgan Caroline, ed. *Italian Canadian*

Voices: An Anthology of Poetry and Prose (1946–1983).
Oakville: Mosaic Press, 1984.

Harney, Robert F. *From the Shores of Hardship:
Italians in Canada.* Welland: Soleil Publishing, 1993.

Hesse, Jurgen, ed. *Voices of Change: Immigrant Writers
Speak Out.* Vancouver: Arsenal Pulp Press, 1990.

Hutcheon, Linda, and Marion Richmond, eds. *Other
Solitudes: Canadian Multicultural Fictions.* Toronto:
Oxford University Press, 1990.

Iacovetta, Franca, Paula Draper and Robert Ventresca,
eds. *A Nation of Immigrants: Women, Workers, and Com-
munities in Canadian History, 1840s–1960s.* Toronto:
University of Toronto Press, 1998.

Jansen, J. Clifford. *Italians in a Multicultural Canada.*
New York: Edwin Mellen Press, 1988.

Kamboureli, Smaro, ed. *Making a Difference:
Canadian Multicultural Literature.* Toronto: Oxford
University Press, 1996.

Karpinski, Eva C., ed. *Pens of Many Colours: A
Canadian Reader.* Toronto: Harcourt Brace, 1993.

Minni, C.D., ed. *Ricordi, Things Remembered: An
Anthology of Short Stories.* Toronto: Guernica, 1989.

Paci, T.G. *Black Blood.* Ottawa: Oberon Press, 1991.

Paci, T.G. *Black Madonna.* Ottawa: Oberon Press, 1982.

Perin, Roberto, and Franc Sturino, eds. *Arrangiarsi:*

The Italian Immigration Experience in Canada. Toronto: Guernica, 1992.

Potestio, John, and Antonio Pucci, eds. *The Italian Immigrant Experience.* Thunder Bay: Canadian Italian Historical Association, 1988.

Ramirez, Bruno. *The Italians in Canada.* Ottawa: Canadian Historical Association, 1989.

Salvatore, Filippo. *Ancient Memories, Modern Identities: Italian Roots in Contemporary Canadian Authors.* Toronto: Guernica, 1999.

Tamburri, Anthony Julian. *To Hyphenate or Not to Hyphenate: The Italian-American Writer.* Toronto: Guernica, 1991.

Verdicchio, Pasquale. *Devils in Paradise: Writings on Post-Emigrant Culture.* Toronto: Guernica, 1997.

WRITING ON AND BY ITALIAN WOMEN

Bona, Mary Jo, ed. *The Voices We Carry: Recent Italian-American Women's Fiction.* Toronto: Guernica, 1994.

Ciatu, Nzula Angelita, Domenica Dileo, and Gabriella Micallef, eds. *Curraggia: Writing by Women of Italian Descent.* Toronto: Women's Press, 1998.

De Franceschi, Marisa, ed. *Pillars of Lace: The Anthology of Italian-Canadian Women Writers.* Toronto: Guernica, 1998.

Del Negro, Giovanna. *Looking Through My Mother's Eyes: Life Stories of Nine Italian Immigrant Women in Canada.* Toronto: Guernica, 1997.

Patriarca, Gianna. *Italian Women and Other Tragedies.* Toronto: Guernica, 1994.

Pozzetta, E. George. *Ethnicity and Gender: The Immigrant Woman.* New York: Garland Publishing, 1991.

REGIONAL INTEREST

Culos, Raymond J. *Vancouver's Society of Italians, Vol 1 and 2.* Vancouver: Harbour Publishing, 1998.

Fanella, Antonella. *With Heart and Soul: Calgary's Italian Community.* Calgary: Universiy of Calgary Press, 1999.

Iacovetta, Franca. *Such Hardworking People: Italian Immigrants in Postwar Toronto.* Montreal: McGill-Queen's University Press, 1992.

Taddeo, Antoinette. *Canada, con Passione: A Teacher's Cry for Quebec.* Montreal: Price-Patterson Ltd., 1997.

Trail of Memories:Trail B.C. 1895-1945. Altona, Manitoba: Freisens Corp History Book Division, 1997.

Wood, Patricia K. *Nationalism from the Margins: Italians in Alberta and British Columbia.* Montreal: McGill-Queen's University Press, 2002.

Notes On the Contributors

 **Ivana Barbieri** is a teacher in Toronto. She has recently returned from Spain where she worked as an EFL educational consultant for the British Council in Toledo and Madrid.

Rosanna Battigelli has a double B.A. in Italian and French, and has also studied Spanish, German, and Latin. She began teaching in 1981 and has given workshops on early literacy to teachers across Ontario. She writes fiction for children  and adults. Several of her short stories appear in

Canadian anthologies. Her first novel, *Crossroads*, is set in Canada and Italy in the early '70s, and she is presently researching and writing a historical novel, *La Brigantessa: The Life of a Female Bandit*, based on true events in southern Italy in the 1860s, during a tumultuous period called "The Decade of Fire." She lives in Sudbury.

Angela Capozzolo is a high school teacher and has continued her studies at the University of Toronto, where she has completed a Master of Education degree and a Certificate in Educational Administration. Her latest academic adventures have taken her to the l'Università Per Stranieri in Perugia, Italy. She lives in Toronto.

Maria Cioni took to heart her parents' advice — if you worked hard, you could accomplish anything — and obtained her Ph.D. in history from Cambridge University. She has pursued a career in international education project develop-

ment and negotiation and is currently writing a book on the contribution of her father's Italian restaurants to Calgary's socio-cultural history. She lives in Toronto.

Maria Coletta McLean is a freelance writer for the *Toronto Star* and has been published in the *Globe and Mail*, *Modern Woman*, *The eyeTalian*, and *Accenti*. In 2000, *My Father Came from Italy*, her non-fiction memoir, was published by Raincoast Books. Maria is the president of the family business, Columbia Coffee, and is currently working on a novel. She lives in Toronto. Visit her Web site at www.mariacoletta.com.

Jennifer Febbraro is currently a Ph.D. candidate in the Department of Sociology and Equity Studies at the University of Toronto. She also works as an abstract painter and has had shows across Canada and the U.S. Currently,  she writes as the art critic for *Tandem Magazine*, an Italian cultural newspaper, and teaches Grade 11 English at Central Tech in Toronto.

 **Nancy Kindy** works as a financial planner for a large investment company in Barrie, Ontario, and likes to spend time at her cottage just outside of Burk's Falls, where many stories can be told around the campfire.

Maria Francesca LoDico is a Montreal writer and journalist. She is presently working on a magic-realist novel, *The Giants of Agrigento*, based on her childhood in Sicily, and a memoir about her formidable mother.

 **Carla Maria Lucchetta** is a Vancouver-based freelance journalist and TV producer. She holds an English/Creative Writing degree from York University in Toronto. After a 10-year PR career, she moved to Vancouver to pursue writing. She is a regular feature writer and book critic for the *Globe and Mail*, *Ottawa Citizen*, *Vancouver Sun*, *BC Bookworld*, and others. As well, she teaches PR in Simon Fraser University's Writing and Publishing Continuing Education program.

 **Valerie Sovran Mitchell** recently retired from the provincial public service after a career spanning 25 years and a variety of positions, including her last posting as Public Service Commissioner and Deputy Minister of Multiculturalism and Immigration. She now lives and writes in Victoria, B.C., and is the author of the cookbook *Polenta on the Board: Italian Family Cooking, Abruzzese-Style,* which is distributed by Sandhill Books. She is currently writing a book on *grappa.*

Maria Montini received her Masters of Clinical Science in Speech-Language Pathology from the University of Western Ontario. She is presently employed with the Toronto Catholic District School Board. This is Maria's first foray into the world of writing.

 **Anna Nobile** is a freelance writer and journalist living in Vancouver. She has been published in various journals and anthologies, including *Curaggia: Writing by Women of Italian Descent, Hot & Bothered, The Westender, The Loop Magazine,* and the *Georgia Straight.* She is co-host and co-producer of the weekly program *The Storytelling Show* for Co-op Radio in Vancouver, and her work has also aired on CBC Radio. She has just completed her first novel.

Mirella (Sichirollo) Patzer's short story, *The Holy Lance* won the 2003 Annual Hidden Talents Short Story Contest in Alberta and was published in an anthology entitled *Tall Tales and Short Stories.* Her newest work, a novel of  historical fiction entitled *Heinrich the Fowler,* will be released in early 2005. She is currently at work on a new novel, *Otto the Great* and its sequel, *Adelaide of Burgundy.* She is also preparing to launch All Things Italian Ltd., an online business featuring authentic Italian artisan foods and products imported from Italy. Mirella lives in Cochrane, Alberta, and holds two Management Certificates from the University of Calgary.

 **Luciana Ricciutelli** has been the editor of a feminist academic journal, *Canadian Woman Studies/les cahiers de la femme*, since 1992. She is currently the series editor of a five-volume anthology, *Women, Power and Justice: Global Feminist Perspectives*. The first volume, which she is also co-editing *Feminist Politics, Activism and Vision: Local and Global Challenges* will be published as a joint Zed/Inanna imprint in Fall 2004. She recently moved to the Madawaska Valley where her family runs a small inn, and like her mother before her, offers evening meals featuring fine Italian cuisine.

Netta Rondinelli is a writer and works in public relations in Toronto. She grew up in the diverse community of Rexdale, Ontario. She is currently working on a novel.

 Francesca Schembri completed a Bachelor of Arts in International Languages and History and a Bachelor of Education at York University, and a Master of Arts from the University of Toronto. She is working on her PhD at U of T where she taught Italian and drama. She also taught romance languages at Seneca College. She has published scholarly and literary work in Europe and North America as well as in Canada in *Canadian Woman Studies*, and in the anthologies *Curaggia*, *The Dynamics of Exchange*, *Sparkles in the Sand* and *The Best Poets of the 90s*. She has also published three plays: *A Husband for Mary*, *It's Not Worth It*, and *Everybody to Dinner*. Her work has won the Turiddu Bella prize for Poetry, the Brancati Prize and the Voce D'Oro.

Giselle Signoroni practices school social work with the Toronto Catholic District School Board and is part of the Deaf and Hard of Hearing Team. She co-edits a newsletter for school social workers in Ontario.

 **Carrie-Ann Smith** grew up in Sault Ste. Marie, Ontario, and graduated from Algoma University a year before her mother. After receiving a master's degree in Library and Information Studies from Dalhousie University she joined the Pier 21 Society, a non-profit organization and National Historic Site where she is now Research Librarian and Collection Curator. She writes a column called *Stories from Pier 21* for Citizenship and Immigration Canada and is a regular contributor to the *Seniors' Advocate* and *Panorama Italia*.